David Bermbach

Benchmarking Eventually Consistent Distributed Storage Systems

Benchmarking Eventually Consistent Distributed Storage Systems

by
David Bermbach

Dissertation, Karlsruher Institut für Technologie (KIT)
Fakultät für Wirtschaftswissenschaften
Tag der mündlichen Prüfung: 10. Februar 2014
Referent: Prof. Dr.-Ing. Stefan Tai
Korreferent: Prof. Dr. rer. pol. Hans-Arno Jacobsen

Impressum

Scientific
Publishing

Karlsruher Institut für Technologie (KIT)
KIT Scientific Publishing
Straße am Forum 2
D-76131 Karlsruhe

KIT Scientific Publishing is a registered trademark of Karlsruhe
Institute of Technology. Reprint using the book cover is not allowed.

www.ksp.kit.edu

Print on Demand 2014

ISBN 978-3-7315-0186-2
DOI: 10.5445/KSP/1000039389

Benchmarking Eventually Consistent Distributed Storage Systems

Zur Erlangung des akademischen Grades eines

Doktors der Ingenieurwissenschaften

(Dr.-Ing.)

von der Fakultät für

Wirtschaftswissenschaften

des Karlsruher Instituts für Technologie (KIT)

genehmigte

DISSERTATION

von

Dipl.-Wi.-Ing. David Bermbach

Tag der mündlichen Prüfung: 10. Februar 2014

Referent: Prof. Dr.-Ing. Stefan Tai

Korreferent: Prof. Dr. rer. pol. Hans-Arno Jacobsen

Karlsruhe, 2014

Abstract

Cloud storage services and NoSQL systems, which have recently found widespread adoption, typically offer only "Eventual Consistency", a rather weak guarantee covering a broad range of potential data consistency behavior. The degree of actual (in-)consistency as a service quality, however, is always unknown. To avoid cost of opportunity or actual costs, resulting data inconsistencies have to be resolved within the application layer. Without detailed knowledge on consistency behavior, though, inconsistency handling is inefficient and for some kinds of inconsistency outright impossible.

Furthermore, due to the way consistency behavior impacts applications, consistency as a system quality should also be considered during the selection and deployment optimization of cloud storage offerings and NoSQL systems. This as well as studying the impact of system design decisions on consistency behavior requires the necessary means to analyze consistency behavior of eventually consistent storage systems.

In this work, we present four main contributions to address the problems outlined above: First, we develop novel consistency metrics which describe consistency behavior for all kinds of consistency, in a precise way, without needless aggregation, and in way that is meaningful to application or storage system developers as well as systems researchers.

Second, we identify key influence factors on consistency behavior and combine them into a model of a storage system. We then present two distinct approaches, which predict consistency behavior based on simulations on top of this model.

Third, we also present a set of system benchmarking approaches to accurately determine consistency behavior of eventually consistent distributed storage systems via experiments with actually deployed systems. Results of both simulation and system benchmarking are expressed using our novel set of consistency metrics.

Fourth, building on 15 extensive experiments with actual systems and a multitude of simulation runs, we demonstrate how inconsistencies can be handled more efficiently leveraging these results. For this purpose, we describe based on a use case how inconsistencies can be resolved in application engineering. We also develop a new middleware-based approach which adds additional consistency guarantees externally to the eventually consistent storage system, thus, alleviating complexity for application developers.

Acknowledgements

A dissertation is never a product of solitary work but builds on the work of others and is heavily influenced by fellow researchers. As such, this thesis is, therefore, also a team effort and I would like to use this space for thanking everyone who helped and influenced me while creating this work.

My foremost thanks go to my PhD advisor, Professor Dr. Stefan Tai, who always supported my ideas and continuously offered valuable advice. He was also the person who inspired me to explore the area of distributed systems in the first place. Without him, I would probably never have started working in this field.

I would also like to extend my sincerest thanks to my co-advisor, Professor Dr. Hans-Arno Jacobsen, who offered a lot of much appreciated feedback for my thesis. His advice certainly helped to improve the quality of this work.

The remaining members of my thesis committee, Professor Dr. Andreas Oberweis and Professor Dr. Frank Schultmann, also deserve my gratitude: Thank you for a professional and fair thesis defense. I actually enjoyed the challenge of defending and discussing my work with you and my two advisors.

Beyond these four, I would also like to thank my colleagues who offered valuable feedback for my work during discussions over coffee breaks or during our group retreats and who also participated as co-authors of my papers: Bugra Derre, Robin Fischer, Dr. Christian Janiesch, Dr. Gregory Katsaros, Markus Klems, Tilmann Kopp, Jörn Kuhlenkamp, Alexander Lenk, Michael Menzel, David Müller, Steffen Müller, Professor Dr. Frank Pallas, Dr. Nelly Schuster, Dr. Ulrich Scholten, Raphael Stein, Dr. Erik Wittern and Dr. Christian Zirpins. Thank you also for a good time over the last three years! Further thanks go to Rita Schmidt for professionally and patiently managing all the administrative hassle for our group.

I also want to express my gratitude to the co-authors of the papers this dissertation is based on: Working with you has certainly helped me develop the ideas of this thesis. Beyond the people already named, these are Dr. Sherif Sakr and Dr. Liang Zhao.

Furthermore, I would like to thank my family and friends who have supported me and who have been patient when I did not have enough time for them. I would also like to express particular gratitude to my father, Professor Dr. Rainer Bermbach, for proofreading this thesis – of course, any mistakes left are still mine.

Finally, I would like to thank anyone who in some way or another helped me with finishing this dissertation - may they be conference participants, anonymous reviewers or someone I have forgotten to mention.

Karlsruhe, 2014
David Bermbach

Contents

Part I.

Foundations

1. Introduction

High availability and resilience to failures are of paramount importance for many applications. Typically, this is achieved by replication, i.e., running several loosely coupled machines with the same application logic concurrently, to assert that at least a subset of the system is available. Replicating stateless machines, i.e., from application and web tier, can be considered a largely solved problem [39, 70]. For stateful machines, on the other hand, replication introduces a new set of problems since state management in distributed storage systems is non-trivial: For instance, consistency trade-offs, as defined by the CAP theorem [45] or the PACELC model [2], have to be considered by developers of distributed storage systems.

This has led to a situation where storage systems from many domains relax consistency guarantees since these weaker – usually eventual – consistency guarantees enable them to run even in large scale deployments with little or no impact on performance and availability. Early examples were distributed file systems [4, 83, 85] focusing on fault-tolerance; more recently, systems for e-commerce applications [37], social media and web search [32, 44, 25, 65], as well as mobile applications [75, 93] have been developed. Today, there are also major cloud storage offerings with relaxed consistency guarantees, e.g., Amazon's S3[1], SimpleDB[2] or DynamoDB[3]. Further examples include big data analytics based on MapReduce [36] and the Hadoop ecosystem's[4] eventually consistent datastores, as well as storage systems for log data and time series analysis from application performance management [80, 3] – relaxed consistency guarantees are omnipresent. Ongoing projects[5] also consider such systems as storage back end for critical infrastructure tasks, e.g., to persist sensor data produced by smart meters or renewable energy plants.

Still, weaker consistency guarantees introduce problems. For example, data is persisted on multiple replicas which are updated asynchronously so that conflicts will occur frequently. Various kinds of failures further aggravate this situation by increasing the severity and frequency of conflicts. Since these conflicts are not handled within the storage system, they are pushed to the application layer where they increase the complexity for application de-

---

[1] aws.amazon.com/s3

[2] aws.amazon.com/simpledb

[3] aws.amazon.com/dynamodb

[4] hadoop.apache.org

[5] peerenergycloud.de

velopers. Imagine the scenario of an e-commerce webshop running on top of an eventually consistent datastore with unknown consistency behavior in the following example:

When a customer selects a product and adds it to his shopping cart, then a later read – either by the same customer or by the webshop application during the check-out process – is *not* guaranteed to return a shopping cart version that contains this product. Similarly, removing a product from the shopping cart is also *not* guaranteed to execute on all replicas right away so that later reads may still return the old version including the product. While the first case will potentially cause cost of opportunity due to customer irritation, the second case will cause actual costs when the webshop provider erroneously sends the undesired product to the customer who will then ask for a refund – including the shipping costs from and to the webshop.

So, if the webshop provider wants to avoid this cost but still use an eventually consistent datastore, he has to handle these inconsistencies within the application logic which is difficult if the degree of inconsistency is not known:

The provider needs to verify that the actual order processed is identical to the one seen by the customer. For this purpose, he might check whether the version stored in the eventually consistent storage system is identical to the one submitted by the customer during the check-out process. Due to asynchronous update propagation in Eventual Consistency (EC), it is unknown *how long* it takes to synchronize all replicas within the storage system and failures may further extend this time interval. Therefore, the webshop provider cannot know when it is safe to process the persisted order. Alternatively, the provider could query all replicas individually before further processing the order – an approach which would lead the concept of storage abstraction and replication transparency ad absurdum.

1.1. Problem Statement

EC is a very popular consistency model which has found widespread adoption in cloud storage services and Not only SQL (NoSQL) systems since it is relatively simple to implement, easy to scale, and does neither impact performance nor availability. Still, EC is a rather fuzzy consistency term covering a broad range of actual consistency behavior so that two eventually consistent storage systems, or even the same system in two different configurations, may behave entirely different consistency-wise. Therefore, the actual degree of (in-)consistency of an eventually consistent storage system is unknown. Combined with the fact that EC also burdens application developers with the complex handling of conflicts and inconsistencies, this unknown behavior significantly aggravates the handling of inconsistencies within the application layer and, therefore, application development. In contrast, a known consistency behavior would enable application developers to more efficiently handle conflicts.

Due to the way consistency behavior impacts applications, it is also desirable to consider consistency as a system quality beyond performance and availability during the selection of a storage system or the optimization of its deployment configuration. Without detailed knowledge on consistency behavior of eventually consistent storage systems, this is not possible. We, therefore, believe it necessary to elevate consistency as a system quality to a level of concern comparable to performance, availability, and cost.

Finally, as EC covers a broad range of consistency behavior, we see room for improvements of consistency behavior without compromising performance or availability by maintaining the same eventually consistent guarantees but changing small aspects of the implementation. Such an approach would lead to a pareto-efficient situation [76] but requires the necessary means to enable systems researchers to study the impact of various system design decisions on consistency behavior.

As such behavior, in contrast to well-studied Quality of Service (QoS) dimensions like latency or throughput, is not directly visible to either storage or application providers, the problem of benchmarking consistency guarantees is non-trivial; there are complex interdependencies of system design, deployment, environmental influence factors and the workloads of client applications which each affect the actual consistency behavior of eventually consistent distributed storage systems.

Due to these issues, currently existing approaches in the area of consistency modeling and simulation [11] have many assumptions which limit them to a small subset of eventually consistent storage systems as well as the prediction of only a few *kinds* of inconsistencies. A generally applicable approach is still missing. Existing approaches for system benchmarking of consistency[6] will not detect all inconsistencies due to the way experiments are set up [98], or use consistency metrics which make their results inapplicable to the problems outlined above [46, 6, 81]. Regarding the efficient handling of inconsistencies there is little work targeting only very specific problem areas [10, 9].

All in all, benchmarking consistency behavior of eventually consistent storage systems is difficult and not even the combination of all current state-of-the-art approaches enables us

- to help application developers handle inconsistencies in an efficient way based on detailed knowledge of the consistency behavior of the eventually consistent storage system used,

---

[6]The term "benchmarking" is a homonym. Within this thesis, we will use the term *benchmarking* to describe the analysis and assessment of consistency behavior using various methods. In contrast, we will use the term *system benchmarking* when referring to the specific analysis method of running experiments with deployed storage systems to determine system quality levels.

- to select eventually consistent storage systems and optimize their configurations and deployments by also considering consistency behavior as a full system quality and, thus, awarding it the appropriate level of attention,

- to study the impact of various system design decisions on consistency behavior with the goal of pareto-efficient system implementations.

1.2. Contributions

We believe that the problems outlined above are best addressed by *Consistency Benchmarking*, i.e., the analysis and prediction of consistency behavior via both modeling and simulation as well as system benchmarking, which can deliver the required information. Suitable approaches can then make use of this information. For this purpose, we present four main contributions within this thesis as detailed in the following sections 1.2.1 to 1.2.4:

1.2.1. Meaningful Consistency Metrics

Benchmarking consistency behavior can deliver information which is useful for the handling of inconsistencies, selection and optimization of storage systems, as well as analysis of the impact of system design decisions on consistency behavior. This, though, requires meaningful consistency metrics that are able to express subtle differences in behavior. Furthermore, there are different consistency perspectives, dimensions and models which we discuss in detail in chapter 2 – consistency metrics need to be able to address all these different kinds of (in-)consistency. Finally, the output of consistency metrics should be meaningful to application developers, storage system developers, and systems researchers, i.e., these metrics should describe consistency behavior in a way that helps them tackle their system problems.

For this purpose, we discuss consistency metrics identified from literature, select appropriate ones and develop new consistency metrics which describe consistency behavior

- for all consistency perspectives, dimensions and models,

- in a precise way,

- without needless aggregation,

- in a way that is meaningful to application developers, storage system developers, and systems researchers.

The identified consistency metrics can be used to express both results of consistency modeling and simulation as well as consistency benchmarking.

1.2.2. Modeling and Simulation of Consistency Behavior

Using a novel set of consistency metrics, we identify key influence factors on consistency behavior of eventually consistent storage systems and combine them into a model of a storage system. We then present two distinct approaches which predict consistency behavior based on simulations running on top of this model.

The presented approach provides the necessary means to run fast and inexpensive simulations to accurately predict data-centric staleness for various deployment configurations. Furthermore, the approach also considers failures and offers at least qualitative predictions for client-centric ordering and staleness. Referring to the example above, our modeling and simulation approach could directly answer the question of how long it takes all replicas of an eventually consistent storage system to synchronize.

1.2.3. System Benchmarking of Consistency Behavior

As a simulation approach is inherently limited in its accuracy to the influence factors covered within the model, we also present system benchmarking approaches to accurately determine consistency behavior of eventually consistent storage systems via experiments. Where our simulation approach requires a certain degree of insight into the storage system, our system benchmarking approaches comprise variants for consistency measurements from both the perspective of the provider and user of an eventually consistent storage system. We also present system benchmarking approaches for different consistency dimensions and models.

To demonstrate the applicability of our system benchmarking approach, we also present the results of 15 experiments with real-world storage systems – ranging from cloud storage services to open-source NoSQL systems.

1.2.4. Inconsistency Handling

To demonstrate how detailed insight into consistency behavior of eventually consistent storage systems can help application developers handle inconsistencies more efficiently, we extend our example from above to comprise typical webshop business operations, and then sketch out how inconsistencies for such a concrete use case can be handled in application engineering.

Some kinds of inconsistencies, especially those caused by concurrent updates, can only be handled in primitive ways outside of the application layer, e.g., by dropping updates or by using simplistic *Last Write Wins* strategies. Application-specific knowledge on the meaning of the conflicting versions, in contrast, allows to resolve these conflicts without loss of information.

All other inconsistencies, i.e., inconsistencies *not* requiring application-specific knowledge, can be resolved without loss of information outside of the application layer. These inconsistencies could, therefore, also be managed within a middleware layer which would then reduce the complexity for application developers. For this purpose, we also present a middleware-based approach which implements client-centric consistency on top of an eventually consistent storage system. In our example above, this middleware component would be useful for the webshop provider by alleviating parts of the complexity of handling inconsistencies.

We also describe possible extensions to this middleware to further increase consistency guarantees externally to the storage system as well as to handle these inconsistencies in a much more efficient way with less overhead.

These four contributions combined increase the transparency and comparability of consistency behavior of eventually consistent storage systems. Thus, they allow system researchers to study the effects on consistency resulting from system design decisions; they also allow application developers to make conscious decisions on the selection and configuration of an eventually consistent storage system, and they remove parts of the complexity of inconsistency handling within the application from the application developer and demonstrate to him, based on an example, how the remaining inconsistencies can be handled by co-design of application and datastore.

1.3. Organization of this Thesis

This thesis contains four parts. Part I, *Foundations*, starts with this chapter and continues with the presentation and discussion of consistency definitions, perspectives and models, trade-offs in distributed state management, select storage systems, and failure types in distributed systems in chapter 2. This Part also contains a discussion of related work in chapter 3.

Part II, *Consistency Benchmarking*, contains the first three main contributions of this work. Building on the initial considerations and related work from Part I, we identify and discuss consistency metrics which can be used to accurately quantify the consistency behavior of eventually consistent storage systems (chapter 4). In chapter 5, we present an approach which abstracts a storage system into a model. This model is then used as a basis for simulations which approximate the consistency behavior of the modeled storage system using the metrics from chapter 4. We also present approaches for system benchmarking of consistency behavior in chapter 6 which use our metrics from chapter 4 to accurately measure consistency behavior on actual system deployments both from a provider and a consumer perspective.

Part III, *Application*, shows that the approaches we presented in Part II both work correctly and are useful in application engineering. For this purpose, we start with the presentation of their proof-of-concept implementations in chapter 7 and demonstrate how to use them in practice. We, then, continue with an evaluation using experiments and simulations in chapter 8. Afterwards, in chapter 9, we describe, based on the use case of a webshop scenario, how inconsistency handling can be done in applications with the help of consistency benchmarking results. Next, we present our middleware approach which guarantees client-centric consistency externally to the eventually consistent storage system and also present extensions for additional guarantees or increased efficiency of inconsistency handling.

Finally, Part IV, *Conclusion*, recapitulates the main points of this dissertation in chapter 10, as well as critically discusses our results and presents an outlook towards potential future research directions in chapter 11.

2. Background

Different research communities have different definitions for the term "consistency". In the communities concerned with (distributed) state management, these are the database and the distributed systems community. In this chapter, we start with discussing the two definitions of these communities and also point out differences, similarities and how those two definitions relate to each other in section 2.1. We also analyze how the concept of transactions relates to those two areas.

Afterwards, we take the distributed systems perspective for the remainder of this work and describe different consistency perspectives (section 2.2.1), dimensions (section 2.2.2) and models (section 2.2.3) which we later on (chapter 4) use to identify relevant and meaningful consistency metrics.

Obviously, there is a reason why not every system offers strict consistency guarantees even though this is the most convenient guarantee for application developers. This reason lies in the consistency trade-offs already mentioned in chapter 1: consistency versus availability and consistency versus latency. We discuss these trade-offs in section 2.3 and also give an outlook on how other quality dimensions might affect consistency directly or indirectly.

Finally, to conclude this chapter, we give a brief overview of Google File System (GFS) (section 2.4.1), Bigtable (section 2.4.2), Dynamo (section 2.4.3), and PNUTS (section 2.4.4), whose design ideas were the basis for most NoSQL systems so that elements of it can be found frequently, as well as discuss different kinds of failures which can occur in distributed systems (section 2.5).

Sections 2.1 and 2.2 of this chapter are based on material previously published in NETYS 2013 [15].

2.1. Consistency Definitions

The term consistency is derived from the Latin word *consistere* which means "standing together" or also "stopping together". Hence, consistency generally describes relationships between items that are somehow connected. When considering consistency of data in a computer science context, a consistent state requires that all relationships between data items and their replicas are as they should be, i.e., that the data representation is correct. This focus on correctness of data representation can be seen in both the database as well as the distributed systems community – but on different levels.

The distributed systems community stresses the aspect of distributed state management, i.e., whether replicas of a data item are identical and in which order updates will be realized. The database community on the other hand comes from an originally non-distributed world. They emphasize the relationship between different data items and often include the implicit assumption that replicas are always identical.

The second difference is the way these communities perceive interaction with the datastore. While the distributed systems community typically analyzes independent operations (abstracted as writes and reads on a single key), database researchers use the concept of transactions comprising several operations that are executed atomically (under defined integrity constraints).

In practice however, these two perspectives are often muddled and concepts are used intermingledly so that a clear separation is not possible [22, p.5]. Often this is also a cause of confusion in scientific discussions [78]. We will, however, in the following discuss both perspectives in their original meaning.

2.1.1. Database Systems and Transactions

Within the database research community, consistency is inseparably tied to the notion of transactions. A typical datastore interaction pattern is, for example, a sequence of reads followed by a sequence of updates or inserts.

For instance, the check-out procedure of an online book store could start with checking whether the requested number of books is on stock. Next, it might assert that the customer's data is already persisted in the database or create a new database entry for him. In the third step, the system will probably create a new order entry, issue the credit card charge, and update the number of books on stock accordingly before terminating the check-out procedure.

Here, problems could arise if another customer starts its check-out process for the same books at a later time but completes faster than the first customer. In this case, a book could be sold several times. Also, if the credit card payment fails, the order should be canceled.

Instead of implementing failure handling for every single database interaction, a transaction is an abstraction that effectively handles these problems as described by the ACID properties:

Atomicity A transaction comprises a group of operations. This group of operations is executed atomically, i.e., all operations execute successfully or the transaction is aborted. Transactions that are aborted appear as if they never happened in that they do not make any changes to the database.

Consistency When a transaction commits, starting from an initial consistent state, it always leaves the database in a consistent state. This means that all integrity constraints (see below) are observed and that the global schema of the database is not violated.

Isolation Isolation describes the degree to which concurrent transactions are aware of each other, e.g., by accessing the same data items. See below for a detailed description of different isolation levels.

Durability A transaction that commits is always durable, i.e., all the changes that the transaction has made become permanently visible to other transactions. Furthermore, the changes are persisted and will never be undone aside of catastrophic system failures where the entire database is compromised.

Hence, the consistency focus of database systems is on the relationships between data items and the overall correctness of the entire database. They can be guaranteed in a distributed setting but it is expensive to do so as consistency and isolation are typically guaranteed via locking mechanisms, e.g., 2-phase locking, which create an extensive communication overhead in a distributed setting. Here, it can be seen that transactions were intended as "a simple programming abstraction to cope with concurrent executions, rather than to address the challenges of a distributed setting." [82].

An in-depth introduction to relational databases is beyond the scope of this dissertation, we refer the interested reader to, e.g., [50].

Integrity Constraints

As originally proposed by Codd [31], consistency means compliance with integrity constraints, i.e., a (relational) database is consistent when all integrity constraints are preserved and transactions are required to always leave a database in a consistent state. Four different kinds of integrity constraints can be distinguished:

Entity Integrity Rows in a relational database are identified by a unique primary key. Entity Integrity specifies that a primary key may never be null, i.e., that there is no row without a key.

Referential Integrity Rows may contain foreign keys that refer to other rows in the same or another table. This is done to represent relationships between data items. Referential Integrity specifies that a foreign key may either be null (implying that no relationship exists or at least that no relationship is known) or the primary key value of some row. There must be a row with that primary key, i.e., a transaction that either deletes a row or changes its primary key need to assert that all references to the old key (or the deleted row) are updated accordingly.

Domain Integrity Items are of a certain type. Domain Integrity mandates that all values contained within a database are of the correct type. This might also include information on whether a value may be null or not. For instance, if within the database schema an item is declared as an integer, then all characters apart from numbers are forbidden.

Column Integrity Column Integrity allows to further restrict constraints specified in the respective Domain Integrity rules, i.e., this is useful to specify subtypes of existing domain types.

User-defined Integrity User-defined Integrity adds additional rules to reflect business requirements of database users. An example could be that the age value of an employee record must not exceed 67.

While all these integrity constraints are preserved, a database is seen as consistent. For the remainder of this work, we will use the term ACID consistency for this understanding of consistency.

Isolation Levels

In theory, an ideal database would process transactions sequentially. To increase performance, though, several transactions may run concurrently while using suitable mechanisms to show the same behavior as if all transactions were executed according to some global serializable order. Effectively, their individual operations will be interleaved by a transaction scheduler.

In this context, isolation describes the degree to which concurrent transactions are aware of each other, i.e., which interleaving of operations are acceptable and which are not. There are several isolation levels ranging from the weakest level, *Read Uncommitted*, to the strictest level, *Serializable* (which is rarely offered in actual products [8]). The ANSI Structured Query Language (SQL) standard knows four levels of isolation:

Read Uncommitted At this isolation level, there is virtually no isolation, i.e., concurrent transactions may see each other's uncommitted updates even though both transactions might still be rolled back at a later point in time. This phenomenon is called dirty read.

Read Committed Here, a lock-based Relational Database Management System (RDBMS) releases all its read locks right after reading. Hence, a value read is always committed but it might not be up-to-date at the time the transaction commits. For instance, a transaction T1 might read a value of 1 for a key k and release its read lock on k afterwards. Next, a transaction T2 might set the value of k to 2 and commit. If T1 now commits, it does so based on the knowledge of of $k = 1$ even though the value has already been changed to $k = 2$. This problem is called non-repeatable read.

Repeatable Read This isolation level mandates that for lock-based implementations all locks are kept until commit time (i.e., in contrast to Read Committed read locks are not released prematurely). This does not preclude, though, that two reads over the course of the same transaction return a different set of values as a concurrent transaction might change rows previously not selected – so that they match the selection criteria for the second read – or insert additional rows that also match the selection criteria. This phenomenon is called phantom reads.

Serializable A database running at an isolation level of Serializable guarantees that its transaction scheduler will interleave concurrent transactions in a way that asserts that the final state of the database is identical to a state where all transactions were executed in some sequential order.

Practical implementations, though, also offer non-standardized isolation levels, e.g., Snapshot Isolation [14].

2.1.2. Distributed Systems

While database researchers see consistency as one of four ACID properties describing integrity constraints in the context of transactions, researchers from the distributed systems community investigate state shared by multiple replicas, i.e., several copies of a datum exist which may or may not be identical. Executions of operations on these replicas may read or change the state at one or more replicas but are typically not transactional. Essentially, "a consistency criterion [or consistency model] defines which executions of a distributed system are considered correct" [48], i.e. which order of operations leaves the data in a correct state. This translates to the issue of "which updates will be visible to which client in which order". I.e., consistency is, from a distributed systems perspective, more comparable to the ACID property isolation which describes when updates will be visible to which concurrent transaction. Both ACID consistency and isolation, on the other hand typically require equality of replicas and chronologically correct operation ordering as a necessary precondition since it is hard to maintain integrity constraints or to guarantee the invisibility of uncommitted updates in the presence of differing replicas.

From a distributed systems perspective, consistency is, hence, about equality of replicas and the ordering of operations[1]. Depending on a concrete *Consistency Model* requiring a particular way of operation ordering, e.g., "execute all operations on all replicas in the same order", an actual execution order of requests may or may not lead to a consistent state. To emphasize, a specific order in which requests are executed may satisfy consistency model *A*

---

[1]Ordering guarantees in this context describe how requests may be reordered on different replicas.

while violating the guarantees of consistency model *B*. Therefore, a system can only be in a consistent state with respect to a specific consistency model.

Based on this, we define the distributed systems perspective on consistency as follows:

> A system is in a consistent state, if all replicas are identical and the ordering guarantees of the specific consistency model are not violated.

We will use this definition of consistency for the remainder of this work.

2.2. Consistency Perspectives, Dimensions and Models

For the distributed systems view on consistency, there are three aspects which need to be considered carefully:

1. A storage system operated by some provider is used by a client, i.e., some application. Here, *Consistency Perspectives* describe the angle from which the two actors or roles[2], client and provider, look at the system. Depending on the perspective, different information is of interest.

2. There are different kinds of inconsistencies which can be abstracted into two basic *Consistency Dimensions*.

3. For one of the dimensions, ordering, there are several *Consistency Models* (and, of course, implementations) both from a client and a provider perspective that describe guarantees of a storage system.

2.2.1. Consistency Perspectives

In a distributed storage system there are two perspectives on consistency [90]: the provider (i.e., the entity responsible for the deployment and operation of a storage system) views the internal state of the system. His focus is on the synchronization processes among replicas and the ordering of operations. Hence, this perspective is called data-centric. The other perspective is the one of a client of the storage system. Here, a client refers to the process that interacts with the storage system which can be any kind of application, middleware or even software running on the end user's machine or mobile device. This client-centric perspective views the system from the outside as a black box. Hence, its focus is on the guarantees of the distributed storage system that could also be captured as part of a service level agreement (SLA). Based on these two perspectives, there are various consistency models either taking

---

[2]The organizational entities running the application and the storage system might be identical, hence, roles is more precise.

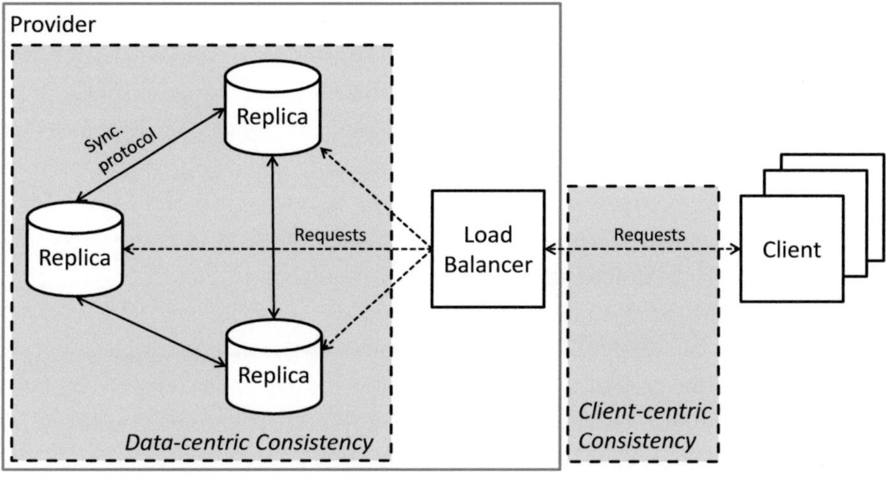

Figure 2.1.: Focus of Data-centric and Client-centric Consistency

a client-centric or data-centric perspective. Still, there is a relation between those models so that some models and combinations thereof mean exactly the same thing while still bearing different names. Figure 2.1 shows the different areas of interest for both the data-centric and the client-centric consistency perspective.

Both perspectives have advantages and disadvantages for the analysis of consistency guarantees – depending on the issue of interest. While data-centric consistency models do not address concrete implementations or algorithms, they certainly describe ordering properties that allow to develop a corresponding synchronization protocol. The downside is that data-centric consistency models are not really helpful to application developers. Client-centric consistency models describe the effects of such a synchronization protocol. While this is very helpful to an application developer, it ignores completely how this could be implemented, i.e., what internal synchronization protocols might deliver such a guarantee.

2.2.2. Consistency Dimensions

Both data-centric and client-centric consistency guarantees have two dimensions: ordering and staleness[3]. Staleness describes how much a given replica is lagging behind, either expressed in terms of time (t-visibility) or versions (k-Staleness)[11]. Again, k-Staleness is

---

[3]Yu and Vahdat[102] propose an additional dimension *numerical error* to describe replica differences based on the semantics of the respective data item. For example, in a warehouse stock management system a numerical error of 10 could describe that replica A sees 10 items on stock while replica B believes this product to be sold out. From our point of view, this is first not always applicable and second a numerical error is essentially a function of ordering, staleness and application access patterns.

a function of t-visibility and the update patterns of the application so that, for application-independent information, t-visibility suffices to characterize the staleness behavior of a storage system. Low, bounded staleness values can often be tolerated by applications as long as the corresponding real-world events would have the same or higher staleness values without an IT system. For example, when person A wires money to person B, the account of A will be charged right away. Person B in contrast might not be credited for some time. In the EU this time window is limited to three days which is far longer than any replica synchronization protocol might take. Hence, small staleness values will often not be noticed.

Ordering on the other hand is more critical. In a setting with strict consistency, all requests must be executed on all replicas in their chronological order which is hard to implement in distributed databases due to clock synchronization issues as the replica servers might disagree on the actual chronological order of events. The standard database mechanism of locking which would solve this problem[4] offers poor performance levels in a distributed setting[5]. Based on this, data-centric consistency models exist that relax certain ordering requirements while keeping those that are essential to applications. These models can be ordered by the "strictness" of their guarantees. Client-centric consistency models take a different approach: While there will almost certainly be cross-effects between the models, the guarantees itself are disjunct in their promises and complement each other.

Figure 2.2 shows an example of commit logs exposing staleness and order error: In the scenario on the left, replica B has not yet received the last two updates that replica A has already committed – it is therefore stale. On the right, both replicas have committed all updates but the last two updates have been serialized in different order on each replica. While this may be acceptable for some consistency models, it is obviously not correct for a strict consistency scenario and shows an example of an order error. Furthermore, this figure can also serve as another hint that ordering is often more critical than staleness: In the scenario on the left, both replicas would return a valid (though possibly stale) version. In contrast, on the right it is not even clear which version is the correct one.

2.2.3. Consistency Models and Implementations

We start by describing client-centric consistency models before continuing to data-centric models and how those two are related. The four client-centric models were originally proposed by Terry et al. [92].

---

[4]First, lock the data item on all replicas; second, update the value; third, release the locks.

[5]In some scenarios, the separation of data and control flow may help to address this problem.

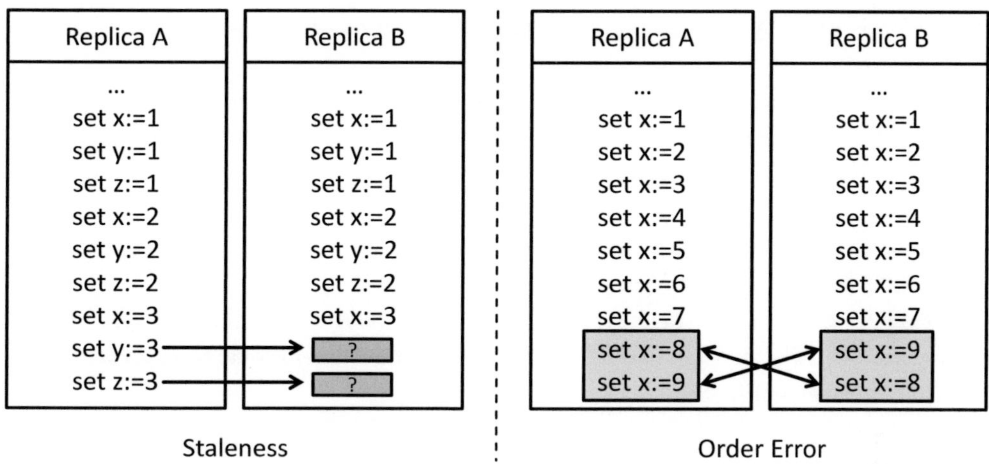

Figure 2.2.: Example for Commit Logs with Staleness (left) and Order Error (right)

Client-centric Consistency

The first model, *Monotonic Read Consistency (MRC)*, guarantees that a client that has read a version n will thereafter always read versions $\geq n$ [90, 97]. This is helpful as from an application perspective data visibility might not be instantaneous but versions at least become visible in chronological order, i.e., the system never "goes backward" in time. For example, imagine person B from our bank scenario above. If this person first sees the credited amount on his bank account statement and then tries to transfer the money to a person C which fails due to "insufficient funds", this will at least cause severe customer irritation if not more.

Read Your Writes Consistency (RYWC) guarantees that a client that has written a version n will thereafter always be able to read a version that is at least as new as n, i.e., $\geq n$ [90, 97]. This helps, for example, to avoid user irritation when person A checks his bank account statement, does not see the transaction and consequently wires the same amount of money again. Generally, RYWC avoids situations where a user or application issues the same request several times because it gets the impression that the request failed the first time. For idempotent operations reissuing requests causes only additional load on the system, while reissuing other requests will create severe inconsistencies.

Monotonic Write Consistency (MWC) guarantees that two updates by the same client will be serialized in the order that they arrive at the storage system [90, 97]. This is useful to avoid seemingly lost updates when an application first writes and then updates a datum but the update is executed before the initial write and is, thus, overwritten. In the bank scenario above, person A might have corrected the account number of person B before finalizing the transfer. If MWC is not guaranteed, the money might end up in the wrong account. According to Vogels [97] "Systems that do not guarantee this level of consistency are notoriously hard to program.".

Write Follows Read Consistency (WFRC) guarantees that an update following a read of version n will only execute on replicas that are at least of version n [90]. This, also, helps (in systems with last write wins strategy) against seemingly lost updates where the update is overwritten by a delayed update request for versions $\leq n$. In all other systems, it reduces the number of version branches. Essentially, this model extends MWC guarantees to updates by other clients that have at least been seen.

In NoSQL and Cloud storage systems, these client-centric properties are typically not guaranteed explicitly but experimental measurements show that they are fulfilled for at least parts of the requests [17, 98].

Data-centric Consistency

In this section, we present data-centric consistency models ordered by the strictness of their guarantees and discuss for each model how it can be translated into a client-centric consistency model. As already discussed, there are two consistency dimensions: staleness and ordering. The following consistency models (apart from Linearizability) do *not* consider staleness [90]. In fact, increasing strictness of ordering guarantees often leads to higher staleness values as updates may not be applied directly but are required to fulfill dependencies first (e.g.,[9]).

The lowest possible ordering guarantee is typically described as *Weak Consistency* [90, 97]. As the name states, guarantees are very weak in that they do not really exist. Essentially, weak consistency translates to a colloquial "replicas might by chance become consistent". While an implementation may or may not have a protocol to synchronize replicas, a typical use case can be found in the context of a browser cache: it is updated from time to time but replicas will rarely (if ever) be consistent. As Weak Consistency does not provide any ordering guarantees at all, there are no corresponding guaranteed client-centric consistency models.

EC is a little stricter: It requires convergence of replicas, i.e., in the absence of updates and failures the system converges towards a consistent state. Updates may be reordered in any way possible and a consistent state is simply defined as all replicas being identical [90, 97]. EC is very vague in terms of concrete guarantees but is very popular for web-based services. Most NoSQL systems implement EC [37, 25, 65, 44].

In terms of client-centric consistency guarantees, EC often fulfills these guarantees for a majority of requests but does not guarantee to do so. As an example, Amazon S3[6] vio-

---

[6]aws.amazon.com/s3

lated MRC in about 12% of all requests in 2011 [17] whereas it only violated MRC with a probability of 5% just one year later.

While there are certainly some use cases where EC cannot be applied, it often suffices as the real world itself is inherently eventually consistent and can often tolerate some inconsistency [101, 91]. The difference is, that conflict resolution is shifted to the application layer [37] requiring a higher skill set from application developers. Instead of pessimistically locking data items "guesses and apologies" are used [49].

Causal Consistency (CC) is the strictest level of consistency that can be achieved in an always available storage system [72] based on the tradeoffs of the CAP theorem (see section 2.3.1). In a causally consistent storage system, all requests that have a causal relationship to another request must be serialized (i.e., executed) in the same order on all replicas while unrelated requests may be serialized in arbitrary order.

A request $r2$ causally depends on a request $r1$

- if both requests are issued by the same client and $r1$ was received at the storage system before $r2$,

- if $r2$ is a read that returns the result of $r1$ which is an update or

- if there is a transitive relation between both requests [90, 97, 23].

Of course, CC captures potential causality so that systems like COPS [71] have to evaluate large dependency trees before applying an update. This both adds an overhead and increases staleness as updates cannot become visible right away. Bailis et al. [9] propose to minimize this impact by having the application explicitly define dependencies that need to be considered. In their follow-up paper [10], Bailis et al. propose a client-side middleware guaranteeing only application-defined dependencies as an alternative to CC. For full CC, a typical implementation uses vector clocks to identify (potential) causal dependencies.

CC can also be defined via the client-centric guarantees discussed above: If all four are fulfilled, the system is causally consistent [23]. It is also possible to create the client-side illusion of CC with the combination of version caching and vector clocks [16].

As Guerraoui and Hari point out, CC does not require replica convergence [48]. Convergence is only asserted when the latest update is causally dependent on all previous writes since the last idempotent replace-update[7] and staleness is bounded. This is also the direct reason why no stronger guarantees can be achieved in an always available storage system: convergence is not required for an update to be successful.

---

[7]i.e., some request like $x := 5$ which does not depend on any previous value.

Sequential Consistency (SC) is a very strict consistency model and cannot be achieved in always available systems[8]. It requires that all requests are serialized in the same order on all replicas and that requests by the same client are executed in the order that they are received by the storage system [90]. While this model does not guarantee anything about the recentness of values read by clients, it mandates that all updates become visible to clients in the same order. Often, SC is described as strict consistency which is not entirely true as staleness is not addressed. But since real-world staleness values are often very small SC usually suffices even for applications seemingly requiring strict consistency.

SC could, for example, be implemented using the Paxos algorithm [67, 68]. Generally, vector clocks that define causal relationships can be in conflict (e.g., for unrelated concurrent updates). If vector clocks are used for request ordering and an approach exists that defines a transitive, global order for all conflicting vector clocks, then a causally consistent system becomes sequentially consistent.

When focusing on client-centric consistency guarantees, the main difference between CC and SC is that WFRC becomes global in so far as reads by all clients are considered. This means that as soon as a client has seen a particular version n, all updates by other clients will only be executed on replicas that have already processed the update to version n. This guarantee can be provided as SC promises that all replicas execute all updates in the same order. So, once a version n has been read, it is assured to have been finally serialized as that version so that any updates will be processed with a higher version number.

Linearizability (LIN) describes what is typically meant with strict consistency. It does not only consider ordering but also staleness, i.e., it requires that all non-concurrent requests are ordered chronologically by their arrival time in the system and that all requests always see the effects of strictly preceding requests. At the same time, all concurrent requests may be reordered arbitrarily as long as SC is preserved. This can be visualized as all operations happening instantaneously at a single point in time between the start and the end of the operation instead of over the course of an interval of time [51].

LIN is hard to implement in distributed systems as there is always the issue of clock synchronization (which is necessary to determine a chronological order of requests for lock-free implementations). In practice, however, sufficiently high precision is achieved to guarantee that violations are highly improbable to occur. Furthermore, in case of violations LIN becomes SC between which applications will rarely notice a difference. While consensus protocols like Paxos [67, 68] can guarantee that all replicas serialize requests in the same order, they cannot guarantee that the order of execution chosen is identical to the actual

---

[8]In CC only requests with causal dependencies must be executed in the same order on all replicas. For SC, this extends to all requests so that replicas need to agree on the ordering of requests for non-causally related requests. This is not possible in the presence of failures so that the system either becomes unavailable or violates its consistency model.

Data-centric Model	MRC	RYWC	MWC	WFRC
Weak Consistency	N/A	N/A	N/A	N/A
Eventual Consistency	Often	Often	Often	Often
Causal Consistency	Single Client	Single Client	Single Client	Single Client
Sequential Consistency	Single Client	Single Client	Single Client	Global
Linearizability	Global	Global	Global	Global

Table 2.1.: Relationship Between Data-centric and Client-centric Consistency Models Ordered by the Strictness of their Guarantees

chronological order of arrival in the system. An implementation using distributed locking, in contrast, is likely to show poor performance.

Expressed in terms of client-centric consistency guarantees, the difference between SC and LIN is that both RYWC and MWC become global properties. This means that a client will always see all committed updates and that all writes will be executed in the (global) chronological order. MRC then also becomes global as a side effect.

Beyond the data-centric consistency models discussed here, there are a few other models (e.g., *PRAM Consistency* which requires that updates by the same client must be visible in correct order, i.e., CC without the last two conditions [24]). We leave these out as, to our knowledge, they have not been implemented in distributed storage systems so that they are currently only of theoretical interest.

Table 2.1 gives an overview of the relationship between different client-centric and data-centric consistency models. Entries "N/A" mean that the guarantee may be reached for single requests from time to time but only based on chance. In contrast, "Often" specifies that such a behavior is seen for a large number of requests. "Single Client" describes that the guarantees as described above (see client-centric guarantees) are fulfilled, whereas we use "Global" to describe when such a guarantee is extended to all clients at the same time.

Other Consistency Models

Beyond the models already discussed, there are also a few other consistency approaches that do not quite fit the categorization used so far.

Multi-dimensional Consistency: In their work on *Continuous Consistency*, Yu and Vahdat [102] introduce the concept of a conit, a consistency unit, which is a three dimensional vector that describes tolerable deviations from LIN along the dimensions staleness, order error and numerical error.

As already mentioned, numerical error is often not applicable and semantically overlaps with staleness and order error. When ignoring numerical error, their work becomes comparable to the work of Torres-Rojas et al., e.g., [95, 96], who coined the term *Timed Consistency*. Timed consistency models are also sometimes known as *Delta Consistency* [88] and essentially describe a combination of ordering and staleness in that the inconsistency window (defined by the time period between the commit of an update and reaching a consistent state according to the ordering model) is bound. This means that the guarantees of a particular consistency model are not reached right away but rather after a fixed period of time Δt. If replicas fail to synchronize during that period of time, the item becomes unavailable until consistency has been reached. This is particularly useful for describing and guaranteeing a Service Level Agreement (SLA) and increases the transparency of the consistency availability trade-off.

Sadly, to our knowledge no implementations of Timed Consistency models exist apart from TACT [102] and the work of Krishnamurthy et al. [63] who guarantee bounds on k-Staleness (based on version count). It is possible, though, to specify a *timed* version for each of the data-centric consistency models where the guarantees become visible before the specified time window is over. In that case, the models discussed above become a special case of their timed equivalent (i.e., with a time window of infinity) which also affects the timeliness of client-centric guarantees.

Coherence: In their original definition, data-centric consistency models provide ordering guarantees for all data items, i.e., in CC, for example, two updates by the same client on two different data items must be serialized in correct order. This also implies that an eventually consistent datastore can only be in a consistent state if all replicas of all data items are identical. Depending on the size of the datastore deployment, this may never be the case and it is also more difficult to coordinate updates on large numbers of servers than for just a few. So, for reasons of scalability it often makes sense to provide the guarantees of the consistency model only per key [32]. In the case of our example above, those two updates could then be executed in arbitrary order, thus, granting more flexibility to the storage system. Guarantees per key often suffice as it is then up to the application developer to persist all items, which need guarantees amongst each other, under the same key.

Those models are named coherence, i.e., eventual coherence, causal coherence, sequential coherence, etc. It is common practice, though, to use consistency for both coherence and consistency models alike. To add some clarity, we propose to add a "per key" prefix if coherence is meant, i.e., per key CC instead of causal coherence, and will do so for the remainder of this work.

Ramakrishnan [82] argues that the "unit of consistency" should also be considered as a continuum where guarantees are not only provided either for the entire data set or for just one key but also for groups of keys like, e.g., the entity groups in Google's Megastore [12].

Adaptable Consistency: Kraska et al. [60] propose *Consistency Rationing* where data items are in a first step clustered based on importance (e.g., for a web shop: credit card numbers versus comments on reviews) into types A, B and C. While types A and C are always handled at LIN or EC respectively, B data continuously changes its consistency requirements based on an external cost function. This means that B data is handled at LIN whenever the costs of inconsistencies exceed the cost of opportunity caused by unavailability or high latencies. Consistency Rationing could, for example, be implemented via the much older GARF library [47].

Chihoub et al. [27, 28] present approaches that allow the user to specify maximum stale read rates or a consistency cost efficiency level as part of SLAs. The system then dynamically uses different consistency levels in Apache Cassandra [65] while guaranteeing the SLAs.

Li et al. [69] propose the concept of *RedBlue Consistency* where operations are broken down into very small commutative suboperations that are then categorized as either red or blue meaning that they are either synchronously or asynchronously replicated while guaranteeing dependencies between suboperations. While Consistency Rationing uses different consistency levels based on the data type, RedBlue Consistency adaptively tunes the consistency level based on the kind of operation.

Consistency Models in Asynchronously Updated Views Jacobsen et al. [54] propose a consistency model with four different levels. This model targets view maintenance in large-scale distributed storage systems where asynchronous, concurrent, out-of-order update propagation for non-idempotent operations is the norm. In their work, the authors describe how changes in a base table can be propagated to a materialized view table using version counters, test-and-set primitives and other mechanisms to achieve the different consistency levels defined within the paper.

In their model, all guarantees are per-key, thus, corresponding to the concept of coherence discussed above. As a basic level, the authors define *Convergence* which requires that all records of the final view table, after an undefined period of time, reflect the state of the final base table. Since any arbitrary state of the base table may be defined as final base table, *Convergence* is identical to EC and requires that all propagated updates will eventually be applied on a per-record basis so that, in the end, the replica in the base table as well as the replica in the view table are "identical", i.e., the final view state is correct. Updates comprising sub-operations that may not be commutative with other concurrent updates need to be applied atomically.

Furthermore, there may be several valid intermediate states of a base table when applying a set of updates, since they use timeline consistency as defined by [32], which is similar to per-key CC. Based on this, they define *Weak Consistency* which requires beyond *Convergence* that for all records in all intermediate views, there must be a potential base table, the state of which they reflect. If *Convergence* is preserved, this can only be violated if the view assumes arbitrary random values before reaching its correct final state or if repeated non-idempotent updates make the view table proceed *beyond* the final view state. Typically, one will expect non-random behavior and means to detect repeated execution of non-idempotent updates in eventually consistent storage systems, so that this level is, in practice, comparable to EC even though the definition of EC does, strictly speaking, not include this guarantee.

The authors also define *Strong Consistency* which requires beyond *Weak Consistency*, that the timeline consistency as defined by the base table also holds for the view table which can only be violated by out-of-order update delivery if *Weak Consistency* is preserved. Under the assumption that all updates originate from the same base table replica, this corresponds to CC. Beyond these three models, the authors also define the concept of *Complete Consistency* which requires that for every base table version, there must be a corresponding view table version. This, the authors claim [54], "is not useful to achieve".

2.3. Consistency Trade-offs

You can't have everything, is a common theme in life. Often, different aspects are in conflict and must be balanced until an equilibrium is reached where it is not possible to improve any aspect without compromising another. Such an equilibrium is called pareto optimality or pareto efficiency [76].

For distributed storage systems, several trade-offs exist – two of them affect consistency directly: Eric Brewer's CAP theorem describes the equilibrium of consistency and availability, while Daniel Abadi's PACELC model extends it to also cover the aspect of latency. Beyond these two trade-offs, which we describe in sections 2.3.1 and 2.3.2, there are also some indirect trade-offs. These indirect trade-offs are caused by direct trade-offs between latency or availability and the respective aspect, which is comparable to the concept of indirect exchange within the theory of money. We describe indirect trade-offs in section 2.3.3 and the concept of BASE in section 2.3.4.

2.3.1. CAP Theorem

In his keynote [22] at the Symposium on Principles of Distributed Computing 2000 (PODC), Eric Brewer presented the CAP theorem, named after the three properties *C*onsistency, *A*vailability and tolerance to network *P*artitions. The theorem says, that it is not possible to have all three properties at the same time. Furthermore, partitions occur all the time so that for distributed systems partitioning tolerance is set as a given which essentially leaves only the choice of consistency and availability[9]. This can be easily explained for both reads and writes:

Imagine a situation with triple replication where one replica is unreachable either due to server error or network connectivity issues. Next, an update arrives at one of the replicas. The system, now, has exactly two options: it can either accept the update, execute it on only two replicas and compromise consistency (i.e., the equality of replicas); or it can reject the update, thus, maintaining consistency, and sacrifice availability.

During reads, the effect of the trade-off is comparable: In the same triple replication scenario as above, a read arrives at one of the available nodes. The system can then either respond with an error (as it cannot read the unavailable replica which might have a newer value) or it may respond with a potentially stale answer reading only the available replicas.

Figure 2.3 shows an example where the replica on the right is unavailable while an update arrives in the replica on the left. The system can then either choose the left path and reject the request or opt for the right path and sacrifice consistency.

Of course, the consistency availability trade-off is a continuum for both reads and writes. In a scenario with again three replicas, the system could respond to requests as long as zero, one or two replicas cannot be reached. This continuum is often used in the context of quorum systems [94] where configurable parameters N, R and W describe the number of replicas (N), the number of replicas which must respond to a read request (R), and the number of replicas which must respond to a successful write request (W). While $R + W > N$ and $W/2 > N$ the system is guaranteed to avoid concurrent updates and to always return the results of the latest write during reads.

In 2002, Gilbert and Lynch [45] formally showed the correctness of the theorem under a set of rigid assumptions.

2.3.2. PACELC Model

In his original 2010 blog post [1] and later on in his follow-up paper [2], Daniel Abadi criticizes a certain asymmetry within the CAP theorem[10]. Furthermore, he points out that the "[...] main problem with CAP is that it focuses everyone on a consistency/availability tradeoff, resulting in a perception that the reason why NoSQL systems give up consistency is to get availability. But this is far from the case." [1].

In practice, systems often sacrifice consistency even while there is no network partitioning, i.e., while they do not seem to need to. This is caused by the second consistency trade-off, consistency versus latency, which can again be seen both during writes and reads.

---

[9]Partitioning tolerance can only be forfeited for non-replicated, single site systems where no partitions can occur.

[10]CP systems (consistent and partitioning-tolerant) and CA systems (consistent and available) are essentially identical, since a network partitioning shows itself typically in unavailability of the system.

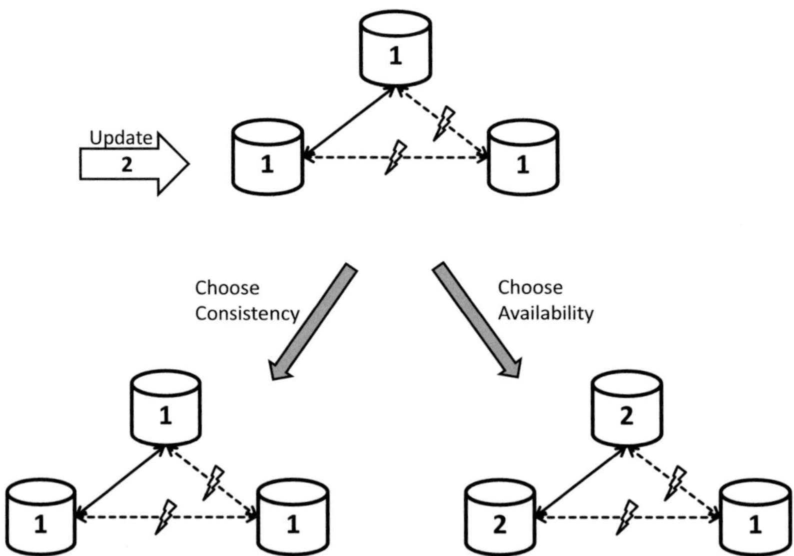

Figure 2.3.: Consistency versus Availability Trade-off During Updates

For example in a scenario with three geographically distributed replicas, it takes some time to propagate updates to all replicas and receive their acknowledgments. System designers can either choose to update all replicas synchronously, and, thus, maintain consistency while accepting high system latencies; or updates can be propagated asynchronously in the background after the operation has already committed. In this case, consistency is sacrificed in favor of low system latencies.

A read in the same scenario could again choose to either only read the closest replica and, thus, opt for latency; or it could wait for responses from all replicas, thus, choosing consistency over latency. Obviously, this is again a continuum, e.g., the request could also terminate after reading two out of three replicas etc. This as well is often used in quorum systems [94].

Figure 2.4 shows an example with two replicas during an update: The system can either choose to have the update propagation delay between replicas 1 and 2 as part of the request latency or as part of the inconsistency window.

The PACELC model is a superset of the CAP theorem: If there is a *P*artition, trade off *A*vailability for *C*onsistency; *E*lse trade off between *L*atency and *C*onsistency [1, 2].

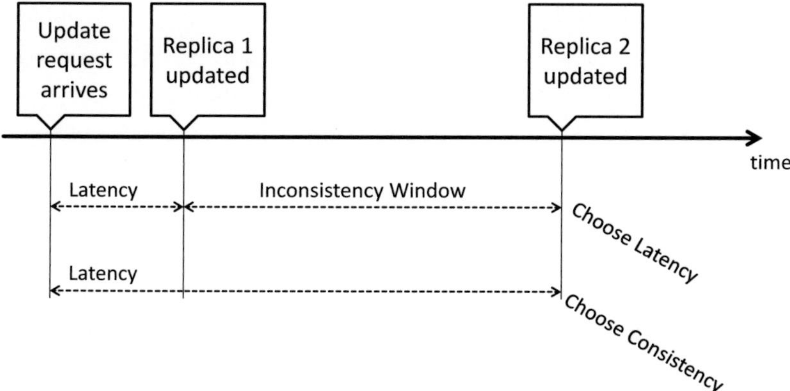

Figure 2.4.: Consistency versus Latency Trade-off During Updates

2.3.3. Indirect Trade-offs

Apart from the trade-offs of the previous two sections, there are other trade-offs that do not affect consistency directly. Indirectly, though, they have an effect. For example, if there is a trade-off between a quality Q and latency. Then it is possible to solve the consistency latency trade-off in a way that favors consistency. Afterwards, Q is then compromised to reduce the latency again, thus, indirectly granting the opportunity to seemingly have good latency and consistency at the same time.

This mechanism is comparable to the economical concept of indirect exchange where two goods are not exchanged directly (e.g., five apples against five bananas) but rather indirectly using an auxiliary vehicle like money (e.g., sell five apples for five Euros and buy five bananas for five Euros).

In the following, we describe some exemplary trade-offs that can be used to enhance latency or availability after it was compromised in favor of consistency or the other way around.

Latency versus Durability Latency and Durability can be traded off, for example, by keeping data either in memory (favoring latency) or writing it to disk (favoring durability). Other influence factors could be using Redundant Array of Independent Disks (RAID) systems at different levels or different disk types.

Latency versus Cost Latency can also be influenced by the amount of money one is willing to pay: Using more (scale out) and better machines as well as more network bandwidth (scale up) increases cost but improves latency. Furthermore, the different storage solutions from the durability trade-off also come with different price tags.

Latency versus Confidentiality Confidentiality typically requires encryption combined with various authentication and authorization mechanisms. All these aspects add a latency overhead so that confidentiality could be compromised to improve latencies and vice versa. This is directly connected to a trade-off between confidentiality and cost [26].

Availability versus Confidentiality Authentication and authorization mechanisms are typically provided by a dedicated service or component which is often run at a centralized system. When this component or service fails, the system can either choose to reject incoming requests or to serve them without authentication or authorization mechanisms, thus, endangering confidentiality.

Availability versus Cost Just like in the case of the latency cost trade-off, availability can also be increased using monetary means. For example, different server types may or may not include redundancy at hardware level to decrease the Mean Time Between Failures (MTBF).

Beyond these, there are also other factors that influence consistency, e.g., the number and geographical distribution of replicas. As these influence factors do not quite fit what we typically see as a "quality"[11], we did not discuss them as trade-offs within this section. We will, though, later in this work use our Consistency Benchmarking contributions to study their effects on consistency.

2.3.4. BASE

While ACID guarantees focus on strict consistency, schema adherence, transactions, etc., the opposite approach relaxes consistency in favor of performance and availability. Correspondingly, applications have to be designed in a way that allows them to deal with the resulting inconsistencies and uncertainty. For instance, reliable message queues can be used to assert that updates arrive at remote replicas or to guarantee some degrees of ACID consistency affecting more than one data item. Systems solving these trade-offs in favor of availability and performance are often referred to as "BASE" – *B*asically *A*vailable, *S*oft state, *E*ventually consistent [79].

2.4. Exemplary Storage Systems

In this section, we give a brief overview of the current NoSQL landscape, focusing on the replication mechanisms. We start with four systems whose original design has heavily influenced other systems. These are GFS in section 2.4.1, Bigtable in section 2.4.2, Dynamo in

---

[11]They are more of a tuning knob or a configuration parameter towards consistency.

section 2.4.3, and PNUTS in section 2.4.4. Afterwards, we describe how these design ideas can be found in other existing systems.

2.4.1. Google File System

The Google File System (GFS), as originally presented by Ghemawat et al. [44], implements a hierarchical keyspace similar to a standard file system where files are split into chunks and distributed over so-called chunkservers which hold the actual replicas. A single dedicated (though shadowed) master server manages the distribution of chunks to chunkservers, i.e., the mapping of the keyspace to actual servers.

To allow the system to scale, control flow and data flow are separated in that clients query the master for chunk locations and afterwards interact with the chunkservers directly without any further involvement of the master server. During updates, having obtained the location of the primary chunkserver, the client sends the data to the primary chunkserver directly which forwards them in a pipeline-like fashion to the other two replicas.

While updates with a byte offset as parameter are supported, the system is optimized for record append operations. Interestingly, there is no concurrency control mechanism, i.e., concurrent updates may partially overwrite each other's data. This also leads to several possible outcomes for an update operation: The results may be consistent/inconsistent and defined/undefined. In this context, consistent means that "all clients will always see the same data, regardless of which replicas they read from." [44], whereas defined means that every possible read will fully reflect the result of an update. Based on this, an update will only be inconsistent as the result of a failure, may be consistent but undefined if two concurrent updates manage to intermingle their fragments while all replicas are still identical, or it may be consistent and defined whenever all replicas are identical and updates are not intermingled with another update. Application developers are encouraged to write self-validating records to solve this problem. Please, note, that this understanding of consistency is comparable but not identical to the distributed systems definition which does, in contrast, not consider partial updates or intermingled records.

2.4.2. Google Bigtable

Bigtable, as presented by Chang et al. [25], is implemented as an additional layer on top of GFS. According to the nomenclature of Kraska and Trushkowsky [62] it offers the functionality of the "record manager". While GFS is optimized for large streaming reads and record appends, Bigtable targets applications that need small random reads, updates in place and structured data storage. For this purpose, a "Bigtable is a sparse, distributed, persistent multi-dimensional sorted map [...] indexed by a row key, a column key, and a timestamp" [25].

Bigtable itself does not replicate data, it just implements a structured data interface, shards data horizontally, and allows atomic single row transactions. These transactions can execute entirely local within the server responsible for the respective row. GFS is then used for replication and redundancy. As each tablet server in Bigtable is the single writer for a set of GFS files, the record appends will always be defined if they are consistent (i.e., no error occured) which eases inconsistency handling.

2.4.3. Amazon Dynamo

Dynamo, as originally presented by DeCandia et al. [37], is in contrast to the Google approaches a quorum-based Peer-to-Peer (P2P) system where all nodes have the same responsibilities. A Dynamo cluster is configured via the parameters N, R and W already mentioned in section 2.3. Again, N specifies the replication level, while R (W) describes the minimum number of nodes which need to participate in a successful read (write). While updates in GFS are forwarded in a pipeline-like fashion from the primary replica to the secondary replicas, in Dynamo an update coordinator broadcasts the update to all other replicas; access is directly via a key[12].

Dynamo uses several other mechanisms that affect consistency and replication:

Sloppy Quorum and Hinted Handoffs In Dynamo, all nodes are part of a ring structure which describes the logical distribution of responsibilities per key, i.e., for every key there are N responsible replicas which are kept as part of a preference list. Beyond these nodes, additional nodes on the ring are added to the end of the preference list which will be used in the case of failures. For example, if replica N is not available during an update, then replica $N+1$ will store the update instead and a Hinted Handoff object, which contains the update and the IDs of nodes N and $N+1$, will be created. Once node N is available again, the Hinted Handoff is resolved and the update is stored on the original node. Essentially, updates are stored on the first N healthy nodes instead of the first N nodes within traditional quorum systems [94].

Vector Clocks Vector Clocks [40] can be used to describe the ordering of operations and are frequently used to implement CC. In the case of Dynamo, though, they are used to identify update conflicts where one version is a predecessor of another version and which can, therefore, be resolved automatically. This is usually the case for all conflicts not caused by concurrent updates.

Merkle Trees Each node keeps a Merkle Tree of the keyrange it is responsible for. A Merkle Tree is built by using hashes of actual data as leaves and hashes of hashes for

---

[12]There is a flat keyspace with consistent hashing as partitioning mechanism.

all other vertices. In the case of Dynamo, this is used to efficiently compare the equality of the entire keyrange (i.e., whether the root vertices of the Merkle Trees are identical) and to quickly identify keys with conflicting values (i.e., traverse the tree branch with the differing values until the responsible key is found). Based on the corresponding vector clocks, the conflict will then be resolved either automatically by the storage system or at application level (due to application datastore co-design) during the next update by returning all existing versions during a read.

2.4.4. Yahoo! PNUTS

Yahoo! PNUTS, as originally presented by Cooper et al. [32], again takes a different approach than Google and Amazon. There are three key differences: First, PNUTS offers stricter consistency guarantees than GFS, Bigtable and Dynamo, i.e., per-key CC; second, based on its design for geo-replicated deployments, it uses a geo-distributed pub/sub system for communication between replicas instead of implementing update propagation within the storage system itself; third, the system offers different consistency options as well as added value primitives like test-and-set to application developers and, thus, also eases client-side handling of inconsistencies.

PNUTS, which is part of Sherpa, is deployed in geo-distributed clusters where each cluster holds a full copy of the entire dataset. As updates in typical web applications tend to originate in the same geographic region, it is no performance impact to assign a distinct master per key. All updates are sent to the master which first writes them to the message broker before committing them locally. The message broker then asserts in-order[13], asynchronous delivery of these updates to all other replicas. This asserts per-key CC, a guarantee termed "per-record timeline consistency" in the original paper [32]. Using different read operations – for instance, READ-LATEST and READ-ANY – enables application developers to make conscious decisions on their consistency and latency requirements. Based on this choice, read requests will be routed to the local PNUTS cluster only or if necessary to other replicas as well, thus, increasing latency.

Within a cluster, storage units persist horizontal shards of an RDBMS-like table structure assigned to them by a tablet controller. Beyond the tablet controller, routers hold a periodically updated copy of the tablet controller's state to send incoming application requests to the appropriate storage unit(s). Each storage unit offers range queries and single-row transactions.

---

[13]Guarantees are only provided per message broker cluster. Since all updates to the same key are processed by the same master replica, this master replica will write all these updates to the same message broker cluster. This in turn guarantees in-order delivery for all updates affecting the same key.

2.4.5. Google Megastore and Spanner

An interesting alternative to the two extremes of NoSQL systems and ACID-compliant RDBMS was developed by Google in 2011 (Megastore [12]) and 2012 (Spanner [34]) respectively.

Megastore implements geo-replication with Paxos [67] on top of Bigtable, i.e., several geo-distributed datacenters each run Bigtable clusters and Megastore replicates over those clusters by using Paxos as consensus protocol. Megastore also introduces the concept of an entity group which is a subset of a table, e.g., the inbox of a single Gmail[14] user. Within this entity group, Megastore offers fully ACID-compliant transactions whereas transactions spanning multiple entity groups are propagated asynchronously (or optionally via the two-phase commit protocol). This can be achieved by mapping entire entity groups onto single rows in Bigtable which offers atomic single row transactions.

Spanner, in contrast, uses high precision clock synchronization, exposed via a new "True-Time API", Paxos, and other mechanisms to implement LIN as well as ACID transactions on top of Colossus, the successor to GFS [41]. The data structure used is similar to RDBMS and even uses a schema but is still very similar to Bigtable.

Both systems can be seen as an example of a new trend trying to bring together the database and distributed systems worlds. The motivation by this can be found in the Spanner paper [34]: "We believe it is better to have application programmers deal with performance problems due to overuse of transactions as bottlenecks arise, rather than always coding around the lack of transactions." – personally, we believe that the main problem in this regard is not actually a need for transactions but rather the complexity of dealing with uncertain degrees of inconsistency as well as the fact that most software developers tend to think, thanks to their educational background, in terms of transactions. The "performance problem" mentioned within the quote can also be found within the Megastore and Spanner papers [12, 34] as these systems obviously solve the tradeoffs of the CAP theorem [45] and the PACELC model [2] in favor of consistency:

- Megastore reports average read latencies of less than 100ms for only around 65% of their production applications – for writes this value is around 600ms. Both kinds of requests show maximum values of around 1000ms.

- Spanner reports average production latencies only for the F1 application: Reads take around 9ms (with very high standard deviation values, though), write transactions have latencies of around 70ms (single-site commit) or 100ms (multi-site commit) respectively.

---

[14]gmail.com

In contrast, other systems clearly favoring low latency and availability report the following performance numbers:

- Lakshman and Malik [65] report for Facebook's Cassandra, running on 2010 hardware, that production latencies in a geo-distributed deployment are between 7ms and 44ms.

- In 2011, Cockcroft and Shean [30] report for a distributed deployment of the (then open-sourced) Cassandra average latencies around 11ms which they claim is comparable to their actual production latencies.

- Cooper et al. [32] report latency values between 60ms and 100ms for PNUTS running on 2008 hardware in a geo-distributed deployment.

- DeCandia et al. [37] report for distributed production deployments of Dynamo average read and write latency values below 5ms. Maximum values are around 70ms. These measurement values were obtained running on 2006 hardware.

While these performance measures are not strictly comparable, they clearly indicate the different design decisions with regards to the CAP theorem and PACELC model. While Megastore offers very poor performance, Spanner has much lower latency values. Nevertheless, *average* Spanner write latencies from 2012 still exceed *maximum* Dynamo latencies from 2006.

2.4.6. Further NoSQL Systems

The design ideas of GFS, Bigtable, PNUTS and Dynamo have helped to spawn a plethora of NoSQL systems. The entire Hadoop ecosystem, for example, is built on top of the Hadoop Distributed File System (HDFS)[15] and HBase[16]. HDFS started as an open source reimplementation of GFS and HBase is originally based on the Bigtable design. Accumulo[17] and Hypertable[18] are also based on the Bigtable design.

Riak[19] and Voldemort[20] originally started as open source reimplementations of Dynamo even though they each have evolved into different directions.

Cassandra[21] is also a very interesting development as it combines elements both from the Google and the Amazon universe by essentially implementing a Bigtable interface on top of a "Dynamo 2.0" architecture. One of the authors of the original Cassandra paper [65] is

---

[15] hadoop.apache.org
[16] hbase.apache.org
[17] accumulo.apacho.org
[18] hypertable.org
[19] basho.com/riak
[20] project-voldemort.com
[21] cassandra.apache.org

also one of the co-authors of the original Dynamo paper [37]. Similarly, DynamoDB[22], an Amazon Web Services offering since January 2012, offers Bigtable-like interfaces on top of the original Dynamo design.

Beyond these, another group of systems tries to reinvent the SQL world and is, therefore, typically referred to as NewSQL [7]. Started by Michael Stonebraker's 2007 paper [89] there is now a new kind of database systems trying to implement classical RDBMS in a scalable way. Examples include VoltDB[23] or NuoDB[24].

Finally, systems like MongoDB[25] or CouchDB[26] implement a new data model where all data is treated as documents. These systems are typically designed as master-slave systems with asynchronous update propagation.

To conclude, the existing NoSQL landscape can either be characterized by their data model (key values store, column or table store, relational store, or document store) or by their replication schemes (GFS-like replication, P2P replication, master-slave replication, Paxos-based replication).

2.5. Failures and Fault Tolerance

In large scale distributed storage systems, failures are unavoidable due to the sheer number of involved machines. To quote a description of the situation at Amazon[27]: "Dealing with failures in an infrastructure comprised of millions of components is our standard mode of operation; there are always a small but significant number of server and network components that are failing at any given time." [37]

Since failures significantly aggravate the frequency and severity of inconsistencies, we provide in this section a short overview of different types of failures (section 2.5.1), the relationship between failures and consistency (section 2.5.2), as well as fault tolerance (section 2.5.3).

2.5.1. Failure Types

Failures in distributed systems can have two main causes: faulty hardware and faulty software. Both types of faults can result in two basic failure types; either the system component is unavailable (crash failures) or does not behave as intended (byzantine failures) [35, p.463]. Coulouris et al. also name "Timing Failures" which are caused by delayed requests. These

---

[22]aws.amazon.com/dynamodb
[23]voltdb.com
[24]nuodb.com
[25]mongodb.org
[26]couchdb.apache.com
[27]amazon.com

failures can, at our level of abstraction, be described as temporary crash failures of the network links. This leaves us with byzantine and crash failures. Beyond these, Özsu and Valduriez [74, p.325] categorize failures regarding a time horizon. According to them, failures can either be "permanent" or "intermittent and transient", i.e., failures can be both temporary or permanent. Based on these two categorizations, this thesis considers three different failures:

Crash-stop Failures During a crash-stop failure, a system component (either parts of the network or a server) is no longer available. Requests are typically lost or queued somewhere else until the component is available again. In the case of crash-stop failures, though, the unavailability is permanent regarding a near time horizon. Hence, a typical action upon this kind of failure will be to replace the failed component.

Crash-recover Failures A crash-recover failure is a transient, non-permanent version of the crash-stop failure. Both failures are often difficult to distinguish at first sight; e.g., a crashed server may have crashed due to a loose power chord (which can be fixed rather quickly) or it may have crashed due to a short-circuit fault somewhere within the machine (which can usually not be fixed right away). Only manual inspection or intervention will typically be able to distinguish both kinds of failures both of which occur frequently in large networks. Some crash-recover failures, e.g., temporary unavailability of network connectivity, will "repair" itself and will, hence, often go completely unnoticed. While this may seem desirable at first sight, it is not as servers may be in an error state without even knowing about it. Additional fault tolerance mechanisms will further mask the failure. This potentially leads to situations where the failures quickly add up until they are finally noticed by the people operating the system. An outage with similar root causes was recently reported by Amazon Web Services [87].

Byzantine Failures A byzantine failure can be caused by either software faults due to bugs, hardware faults (e.g., faulty memory where a single bit has turned), or by security breaches. In either case, the result is the same: The system component does not behave as intended. For instance, a server may respond to requests using either gibberish (which is not as dangerous as it can easily be detected) or using the wrong response, thus, creating an erroneous view of the server's state for the client. Especially the latter case, often caused by a malicious attacker is hard to detect. Many algorithms in distributed systems also have byzantine fault-tolerant equivalents where a number of byzantine faults can be tolerated. These algorithms, though, typically come at high cost as they require interaction with several servers instead of one.

All these failures can occur both isolated or correlated. An extreme example of correlated failures could be a natural disaster wiping out an entire datacenter. In the remainder of this work, we do not consider byzantine failures and exclusively refer to crash failures when discussing failures and behavior caused by failures.

2.5.2. Failures and Consistency

As already discussed in sections 2.3.1 and 2.3.2, there is a direct trade-off between consistency and availability. When systems choose consistency over availability, crash failures typically cause unavailability. But if systems opt for availability instead of consistency, failures typically cause inconsistencies of various types.

For instance, in a scenario with three replicas where replica A is crashed for a period T, replica A will miss all n updates during this period. If the failure were permanent, consistency would not be affected, but if the replica becomes available after the period T, then it depends on whether A communicates with another replica or with a client first. All clients, which read from this replica (assuming just one replica is read) before resynchronization of A with another replica, will observe t-Visibility of about T and k-Staleness of at least n. Depending on the clients' requests before contacting A, MRC, WFRC and RYWC might be violated. If the system does not use mechanisms like vector clocks or other version counters, MWC might be violated as well if a client issued a write to A right before the replica failed and issued another write to replica B during the unavailability. In that case, A might propagate the first update which then would replace the second one, thus, violating MWC.

Generally, crash failures typically cause inconsistencies of all kinds depending on the actual client requests during the period that the problem persists. As soon as the failure is resolved, these inconsistencies become visible to clients if the system does not resynchronize fast enough. Sufficiently fast resynchronization is often difficult as failure detection is a non-trivial issue so that a temporary failed replica might not even realize that it had a failure, hence, requiring resynchronization. Similarly, inconsistencies also become visible if clients interact with different parts of the system during network partitions but still maintain external means of communication, i.e., client A sends an update to system part 1 and tells client B about it. If client B then accesses system part 2, he will not be able to read A's update.

Especially crash-failures of network links (i.e., network partitions) but also of replicas tend to create version branches which are impossible to synchronize within a storage system[28] without information loss.

2.5.3. Fault Tolerance

Özsu and Valduriez [74, p.331] define fault tolerance as follows: "Fault tolerance refers to a system design approach which recognizes that faults will occur; it tries to build mechanisms

---

[28] At least, without application-specific information like within the Ficus File System [83]

into the system so that the faults can be detected and removed or compensated for before they can result in a system failure.". Most mechanisms fall in the areas of redundancy and/or modularization [74, p.331], i.e., having several identical instances with well-defined input and output interfaces that are implemented as independent of each other (and other modules as well) as possible.

A good example for modularization and redundancy is the Paxos algorithm [67, 68]: Each participating role (proposer, acceptor, learner) can be assumed by more than one machine (redundancy) which communicate via well-defined interfaces (modularization). For decisions, only a majority of acceptors is required, i.e., ideally only one machine beyond a 50% quorum must be available. Using asynchronous messaging for communication further increases the modularization and independence of machines. There is also a Paxos variant which can tolerate byzantine failures.

2.6. Conclusion

In this chapter, we started by describing different definitions of consistency from a database or distributed systems view. We then focused on the distributed systems view and discussed consistency perspectives (client-centric and data-centric), consistency dimensions (staleness and ordering), as well as different consistency models both from a client (MRC, RYWC, MWC, WFRC) and provider perspective (LIN, SC, CC, EC, Weak Consistency).

In the third part of this chapter, we discussed consistency trade-offs, namely consistency versus latency and availability, as described by the CAP theorem and the PACELC model. We also covered the concept of indirect consistency trade-offs.

Finally, we presented four influential NoSQL systems (GFS, Bigtable, Dynamo, and PNUTS) and briefly discussed the NoSQL landscape as well as typical failure and fault tolerance scenarios in distributed storage systems.

3. Related Work

Our work proposes a set of novel ideas and approaches that for the first time cover the field of Consistency Benchmarking and the use of its results as a whole. In this chapter, we, therefore, discuss related approaches for each main contribution in separate sections, starting with work on modeling and simulation of arbitrary QoS attributes in section 3.1. Next, in section 3.2 we describe existing approaches for system benchmarking of distributed storage systems. Finally, before coming to a conclusion, we discuss approaches which are concerned with the management of consistency in distributed storage systems in section 3.3.

More basic literature which our approaches build upon can also be found in chapter 2 which we do not fully recap within this chapter. We also do not discuss related work on consistency metrics here as we use chapter 4 to identify requirements for consistency metrics first before discussing metrics from related work with regards to these requirements.

This chapter reuses material previously published in MW4SOC 2011 [17], TPCTC 2013 [19], IC2E 2013 [16], NETYS 2013 [15], and IC2E 2014 [18].

3.1. Modeling and Simulation of Software Quality

There is a lot of work on performance prediction mainly from the software engineering community [13, 100, 52, 59, 38], to name just a few examples. To our knowledge, however, none of these address consistency of distributed storage systems – either because the focus is more on non-distributed systems or on distributed queuing system. This is probably due to the fact that strict consistency was considered a given in classical database systems, where only a few research prototypes dared to relax consistency, e.g., [85, 83, 93, 64, 4]. Only with the advent of large scale web applications and the success of Cloud Computing, has EC found more widespread adoption [25, 32, 37, 44, 65, 12]. This is because the CAP theorem [45] and the PACELC model [2] call for relaxed consistency guarantees for those systems or rather in those use cases where neither reduced availability nor high latencies can be afforded.

Bailis et al. [11] also propose to simulate consistency behavior in distributed storage systems. They present a model called WARS coupled with Monte Carlo simulations. In contrast to our model, as we will see in chapter 5, their approach is limited to Dynamo-style [37] quorum systems using *Last Write Wins* as a conflict resolution strategy while our approach allows for arbitrary replication schemes – in that regard their model is essentially a subset of ours. To our understanding, their model assumes identical distributions of network link latencies between *all* replicas, i.e., their approach can only work for replicas in single site, non-geo-distributed deployments which will show similar (low) latencies between all replicas. Furthermore, they consider neither failures nor ordering or client-centric consistency behavior. So, while, at a first glance, their approach seems similar to our contribution from chapter 5, there are a few key differences.

3.2. System Benchmarking of Distributed Storage Systems

There is a lot of work on system benchmarking of distributed storage systems, e.g., [33, 104, 58, 20, 43, 80, 73]. Some of those even call for system benchmarking of consistency behavior in their future work section but neither of them addresses the issue itself.

Wada et al. [98] propose an approach to experimentally determine client-centric consistency behavior of distributed storage systems with only black box access (i.e., a get and put interface and no further knowledge on the system internals). As this approach uses only a single machine for reading and writing, many inconsistencies will go unnoticed by their approach. Essentially, it is more comparable to our approach for RYWC measurements than to our staleness measurements which we will both present in chapter 6. This can also be seen in the fact that in their experiments they are not able to observe the (at that time) really surprising staleness patterns in Amazon S3. Still, we see their work as a basis for our system benchmarking approach. We have later extended and modified it in joint work with Stefan Tai [17], as well as with Liang Zhao and Sherif Sakr [19].

Anderson et al. [6], Golab et al. [46], and Rahman et al. [81] of HP Labs present an alternative approach using metrics based on Lamport's definitions of safeness, regularity, and atomicity [66]. These definitions stem from the synchronization of processes in multi-core systems. As access times to the main memory are very low, staleness values are, in the original scenario, negligible which is entirely different in distributed storage systems. Furthermore, each of these metrics aggregates the staleness and ordering dimensions so that we believe that they cannot provide meaningful results for any of the problems which we identified in chapter 1. In chapter 4, we will discuss several key requirements for consistency metrics based on literature and IEEE standards – due to the aggregations used, their metrics violate several of these requirements. Additionally, their metrics capture only maximum deviations so that they are best used for systems showing very low variance in consistency behavior which, as we have seen in our experiments, is rarely if ever the case in eventually consistent storage systems. In their experiments, they measure inconsistencies observable in actual application workloads. While this may seem desirable at a first glance, this mainly detects inconsistencies caused by the application workload instead of inconsistencies caused by the storage system implementation. In our discussion section of chapter 7, we will explain in detail why this is the case.

Zellag and Kemme [103] also present an alternative approach counting consistency anomalies for arbitrary cloud-based applications in transactional and non-transactional datastores. At runtime, their approach builds a dependency graph to detect cycles, i.e., consistency violations. To our knowledge, their approach is currently limited to storage systems offering at least CC which is typically not supported by cloud storage services or NoSQL system.

Patil et al. [77] also measure staleness in terms of time within their implementation of YCSB++ extending the original YCSB [33] system benchmark. Their approach, though, can only measure rough approximations of actual consistency behavior due to the way values are measured.

Klems et al. [57] also propose consistency system benchmarks but their approach using Fox and Brewer's harvest and yield metrics [42] does not consider staleness of results, rather measuring availability and completeness of answers of a distributed queueing system. Their results are, hence, not directly applicable to distributed storage systems.

3.3. Management of Consistency Guarantees

There is very little work on handling inconsistencies of storage systems outside said storage system: MDCC [61] uses a client-side middleware component, implemented as a library, to increase the consistency guarantees of an eventually consistent storage systen. For this purpose, they use Generalized Paxos which comes with a price, though: As the middleware components need to communicate, this directly affects latency and under adverse conditions availability. Megastore [12] is implemented on top of Google BigTable [25] to increase its consistency guarantees via 2PC and Paxos. Both approaches end up being storage systems itself instead of just a middleware layer running in a decentralized way. Both systems opt for SC guarantees which have a much higher impact on performance and availability than CC guarantees, which we will later propose in our approach, but might be an alternative if even stronger consistency guarantees are required.

Consistency Rationing [84, 60] is concerned with the adaption of consistency guarantees based on application requirements at runtime. This can either be done by running approaches like our middleware (chapter 9), or using Consistency Benchmarking results (chapters 5 and 6) together with a storage system that offers various consistency settings, e.g., Cassandra [65], or by using storage systems that offer bounds on different consistency dimensions. In the latter category, Krishnamurty et al. [63] propose an approach which allows clients to specify consistency requirements for operations but focuses on staleness. Yu and Vahdat [102] introduce the notion of a *Conit*, a consistency unit, with the three dimensions staleness, order error and numerical error. Their prototype allows clients to specify bounds on each of the dimensions.

Brantner et al.'s implementation of a database on top of Amazon S3 [21] adds database features on top of the key-value store S3. They address consistency only as a sidenote: If MRC and RYWC are desired additional metadata is used to identify inconsistencies and to refetch data in case of violations. This cannot guarantee client-centric consistency but can at least identify violations.

Bailis et al.'s Bolt-on CC [10] can be seen as an alternative approach to what we will present in chapter 9: While our approach can only provide per-key guarantees, their approach offers multi-key guarantees. In contrast to our approach, though, they only capture dependencies explicitly specified by applications which is not identical to CC so that the publication title seems misleading. They also "maximize" staleness by reading only locally from the cache and incur high performance overheads. Furthermore, their approach requires detailed knowledge on the conflict resolution strategy of the datastore which makes it inapplicable for use with most cloud storage services.

Part II.

Consistency Benchmarking

Under "Consistency Benchmarking", we understand the analysis of distributed storage systems in terms of their consistency guarantees and actual behavior. This can be done either analytically by identifying key influence factors in a model and running simulations, or we can use system benchmarking to actually measure behavior of a deployed storage system.

Both approaches have advantages and disadvantages. While system benchmarking delivers accurate results, it requires time-consuming and expensive experimental measurements. Depending on the number of configurations that are of interest, system benchmarking may, hence, not be an option. Simulations, in contrast, require only very little input data which can be reused for a large number of configuration options. Based on an input model, a simulation then delivers approximations or estimates of actual consistency behavior; it does not even require to set up an actual storage system. But while simulations provide results for a fraction of the cost of actual system benchmarks, these results can only be approximations and need to be verified experimentally.

We, therefore, propose to combine the strengths of both approaches by simulating in a first step all relevant configurations and systems. In a second step, we propose to verify the simulated findings for only a few selected configuration options. This approach minimizes cost as irrelevant configurations are not experimentally benchmarked in the first place. To avoid missing promising candidates, though, this requires a sufficiently precise simulation approach. In chapter 5 we present such a consistency simulation approach which works well in concert with the system benchmarking approach for consistency which we show directly afterwards in chapter 6.

This part, therefore, starts with the presentation of consistency metrics in chapter 4 before continuing to, first, consistency modeling and simulation and, second, approaches for system benchmarking of consistency behavior.

4. Consistency Metrics

In this chapter, we discuss different metrics which can be used to quantify consistency behavior of distributed storage systems. We start by describing general aspects of metrics and develop requirements for consistency metrics in section 4.1. Afterwards, in sections 4.2 and 4.3, we describe existing and new metrics for measuring data-centric and client-centric consistency. We also discuss to which degree each of these metrics fulfills the requirements from section 4.1 and identify the consistency metrics which we use for the remainder of this work.

This chapter is based on material previously published in NETYS 2013 [15]. It also includes ideas which were published in MW4SOC 2011 [17] and TPCTC 2013 [19].

4.1. Requirements for Consistency Metrics

Kaner and Bond [55] define, based on the IEEE Standard 1061 [53], an *attribute* as "a measurable property [...] of an entity", i.e., of a quality, while a metric is "the function that assigns a value to the attribute". This function also includes a unit. So, when measuring a certain aspect, a measurement always comprises a value and a corresponding unit (e.g., for the height of a building this could be the value "50" and the unit "meter"). If it is for a particular metric not possible to find two values which do not have any value in between them, the metric is continuous. Otherwise the metric is discrete. An example for a continuous metric would be the height of a person, whereas clothing sizes are an example for a discrete metric.

The overall goal of a metric is to provide a meaningful and accurate representation of the quality under consideration. Based on this, consistency metrics need to be meaningful to either or both providers and clients of a storage system and need to be able to adequately discriminate between different consistency levels. Kaner and Bond [55] further specify accuracy and require the following aspects (we only report the ones applicable to consistency metrics):

Correlation According to Kaner and Bond [55], there should be a linear correlation between the observed attribute and the metric output. As consistency cannot be grasped or measured directly, we propose for our purposes to demand some (not necessarily linear) correlation between consistency and the metric output, i.e., changes in the consistency behavior should be visible in the metric output.

Tracking If the quality changes over time, the metric output should change as well and do
so quickly.

Monotonicity The metric function $M : q \to M(q)$, which maps quality levels q to measurement values $M(q)$, should be a monotonic function, i.e., if q increases $M(q)$ may not
decrease[1].

Discriminative Power The metric should be able to clearly differentiate between low and
high quality levels.

Reliability "The metric shall demonstrate [...(these)] properties for at least P% of the application of the metric." [55]

All of this leads us to the following requirements:

1. Reliability obviously requires *reproducibility*, i.e., measuring the exact same situation
   more than once should yield approximately the same measurement result every time.

2. A metric should preferably be either continuous or at least have a large, expressive set
   of potential output values, i.e., the *resolution* of the metric should be sufficiently high
   and should not contain unnecessary aggregation – otherwise Correlation, Tracking,
   Monotonicity and Discriminative Power might be compromised. Specifically, if aggregation is necessary, it should use short time windows for aggregation (e.g., moving
   averages instead of average) so as not to violate Tracking.

3. A metric should be *fine-grained* (instead of coarse-grained), i.e., it should only measure
   one attribute at a time. Otherwise, two attributes might offset each others effect on the
   metric output. [53] also calls this a "direct metric".

4. A metric may have a target audience but there must be at least one target audience for
   which the results are *meaningful* in that they can actually use them for their purposes.

4.2. Data-centric Consistency Metrics

We now use the requirements from the previous section to discuss the suitability of data-centric consistency metrics.

---

[1] Kaner and Bond name this requirement "consistency". We use the term "monotonicity" instead, which both does
not create another wording conflict as well as serves better to describe the requirement.

4.2.1. Consistency Anomalies

Zellag and Kemme [103] extend their previous work on transactional data stores to non-transactional data stores. They propose to build a global dependency graph based on operation logs and count cycles in the graph as a metric for "consistency anomalies". This is a discrete, coarse-grained metric and one of their main assumptions is that the storage system guarantees at least CC which is very restrictive and does not allow to analyze consistency guarantees of most NoSQL systems which only offer EC. Measurements should be reproducible if the measurement setup can be reproduced but we are unsure who the intended target audience may be. We, therefore, believe that this metric is only applicable for a small range of systems.

4.2.2. Atomicity, Regularity, Safeness

Rahman et al. [81], Golab et al. [46] and Anderson et al. [6] at Hewlett Packard Labs also propose to build dependency graphs based on operation logs and to count cycles in the graph as a metric for consistency behavior. They distinguish the three properties safeness, regularity and atomicity, based on Lamport [66], for which they each count violations. A storage system that has no cycles in its atomicity graph fulfills LIN. The other two properties, though, also consider staleness as well as ordering. Regularity is, thus, stricter than SC whereas Safeness cannot be compared to existing consistency models. Regularity mandates that "a read not concurrent with any writes returns the value of the most recent write, and a read concurrent with some writes returns either the value of the most recent write, or the value of one of the concurrent writes" [6]. Safeness in contrast relaxes the last requirement so that reads concurrent with writes may return arbitrary values. Essentially, safeness requires LIN for non-concurrent requests and Weak Consistency for concurrent requests. Thus, the practical use of this is doubtful as a real-world systems may or may not return the value of the most recent write but, to our knowledge, no system exists that actually returns values that have never been written.

Golab et al. [46] extend these definitions to k-Atomicity, Δ-Atomicity, k-Regularity, Δ-Regularity, k-Safeness and Δ-Safeness. Over an entire set of executions, k-Atomicity reports the maximum version lag encountered during an atomicity violation while Δ-Atomicity measures the maximum time staleness encountered during a violation (likewise for the other four metrics).

The definitions of safeness, regularity and atomicity originally stem from the area of multiprocessor systems [66] where atomicity can easily be achieved as staleness is close to zero since all processes run on the same host. We believe, though, that these three definitions are not very useful in the context of distributed systems. Chockler et al. [29] seem to share that opinion. Still, the theoretical computer science community usually uses these definitions to express consistency in distributed state management.

For all these metrics, reproducibility should be fulfilled if the exact same situation can be reproduced. The measurement resolution, though, is very poor as only the single maximum inconsistency value is reported. Additionally, all six metrics are rather coarse-grained as they measure staleness and ordering at the same time. A practical use beyond theoretical considerations, due to the limitations outlined above, is doubtful: What does it mean to a storage provider or an application developer if a system is, e.g., 5-atomic? The authors yet have to proof a practical use of their results beyond the ranking of systems. Specifically, these measurements are orthogonal to the consistency models presented in chapter 2.

4.2.3. Data-centric t-Visibility, k-Staleness

We propose to measure staleness both in terms of time and operation count/missed versions[2]. t-Visibility describes staleness in terms of time and reports the distribution function of inconsistency windows, i.e., for a large number of executions it outputs the likelihood of a specific inconsistency window length. We define the data-centric inconsistency window as the time interval between the end of a write on the first replica and the end of a write on the last replica.

Measurements of t-Visibility are reproducible as they rely not on a single measurement but instead report a distribution function of staleness values. As arbitrary distribution functions are possible, t-Visibility is a continuous metric and it is also fine-grained as it only measures staleness without ordering. Therefore, it is also completely workload-independent as long as the system is not overloaded. t-Visibility is of interest for storage providers as it gives detailed insight into how long replicas take to synchronize after an update.

k-Staleness, on the other hand, measures how many versions a specific read was lagging behind (also reported as a distribution function). Hence, it also depends on the actual system workload, e.g., in a situation where t-Visibility is at a constant level of five seconds k-Staleness may be between two and three if updates are issued every two seconds. If updates are issued only every ten seconds, though, k-Staleness will be between zero and one. As it can easily be measured as a side product of t-Visibility measurements without additional effort, it can still be useful, though.

For measurements of k-Staleness the same limitations (as for the metrics from sections 4.2.1 and 4.2.2) hold regarding reproducibility: Measurements can only be reproduced if it is possible to reproduce the exact same workload again. As in the case of t-Visibility the metric is continuous and relatively fine-grained even though it depends on the client workload. k-

---

[2]We use the names proposed by Bailis et al. [11] after our original paper [17] had been published.

Staleness is meaningful to storage providers interested, for example, in offering bounds on version-based staleness as part of an SLA.

Bailis et al. [11] also use the metrics t-Visibility and k-Staleness to provide bounds on consistency.

Depending on the storage system's guarantees towards dirty reads[3], the definition of t-Visibility may differ. If a system guarantees no dirty reads, we define t-Visibility without Dirty Reads as the time window between the commit of an update and the end of a write on the last replica. This is identical to t-Visibility with Dirty Reads minus the request latency. In eventually consistent systems, dirty reads are the default case; we will, hence, for the remainder of this work use the term t-Visibility exclusively to refer to t-Visibility with Dirty Reads and will indicate it where not.

4.2.4. Ordering Violations

We propose to measure ordering violations by analyzing the replicas' operation logs to determine the number of violations for the next stronger consistency model; i.e., in a SC system violations of LIN will be counted, in a CC system those of SC and in an EC system violations of CC. Ordering can then be reported as number of violations of consistency model X per unit of time or as a likelihood of violation by calculating the percentage of violating operations.

This metric, obviously, highly depends on the distribution of requests regarding time, target key, originator and kind (read, insert, update, delete). Hence, for reproducibility, it is a hard requirement to replay exactly the same client workload which will often be problematic[4]. Ordering Violations is a continuous metric which is as fine-grained as possible[5]; its measurements are meaningful as they allow to reason, based on a particular workload and certain consistency model requirements, which storage system is able to fulfill these requirements. For instance, if CC is required and the measurements show only a few Ordering Violations of CC in an EC system, then this system might also be an option instead of CC systems which potentially have poorer latency values while being more expensive.

4.3. Client-centric Consistency Metrics

Most researchers so far tend to take the data-centric provider view on consistency, very little work exists on client-centric metrics even though those are highly relevant to application de-

---

[3]Reading yet uncommitted data

[4]This is a common problem for consistency metrics: Ordering cannot be considered without analysis of the request workload.

[5]The dependency on actual workloads is problematic in this context and violations of LIN obviously also consider staleness.

velopers. We now use the requirements from section 4.1 to discuss the suitability of existing client-centric consistency metrics and also propose new ones.

4.3.1. Client-centric t-Visibility, k-Staleness

Wada et al. [98] propose to take a client-centric perspective for measuring consistency. They implicitly define a metric for staleness in terms of time. This metric measures the client-observable inconsistency window as the probability of reading fresh versus stale data over time. Client-centric t-Visibility[6], on the other hand, is defined similar to its data-centric equivalent as the distribution function of inconsistency windows. From a client perspective, we define an inconsistency window as the time between the commit timestamp and the latest possible read of the previous version for systems that do not expose dirty reads. For all other systems, where dirty reads are possible, the inconsistency window already starts with the beginning of the update request, i.e., the request latency is treated as part of the inconsistency window. Again, we will refer to t-Visibility with Dirty Reads when using the term t-Visibiliy as the default case in eventually consistent storage systems. In all other cases we will use the term t-Visibility without Dirty Reads, see figure 4.1 for an overview of the four client-centric and data-centric t-Visibility metrics using the example of a (3,2,1) quorum system[7]. The probability of reading fresh versus stale data over time is a different representation of t-Visibility; transformation is possible in either direction.

Patil et al. [77] also use a staleness metric similar to our definition of t-Visibility [17].

Client-centric t-Visibility generates reproducible results as it relies on a large number of single measurements to create a distribution function. As its data-centric counterpart, it is a continuous metric and it is meaningful for application developers who can, for example, use the knowledge on t-Visibility to determine the time for which the results of issued update requests need to be cached.

As in the case of data-centric k-Staleness, client-centric k-Staleness measures the staleness in terms of versions. The difference is that the client-centric version only analyzes the client-visible version lags. Hence, the metric is not workload-independent but can be measured as a side product of t-Visibility. So, measurements can only be reproduced if it is possible to reproduce the exact same workload again and the metric is continuous and relatively fine-grained. The results are meaningful for application developers, e.g., when trying to prove bounds on how many versions a read might lag behind.

---

[6]We again use the names proposed by Bailis et al. [11] after our original paper [17] had been published.

[7]There are three replicas out of which two will be read during a read. During updates, the operation commits after writing one replica, afterwards the update is propagated asynchronously to the remaining two replicas.

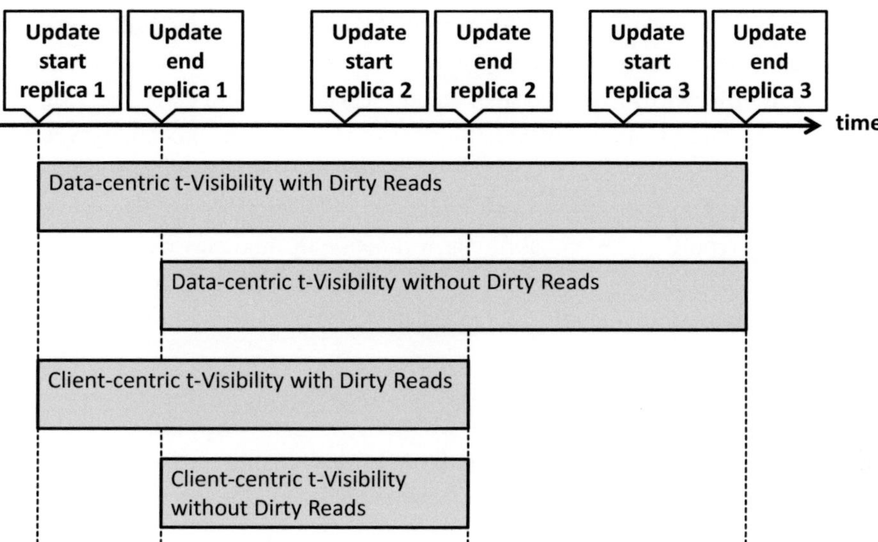

Figure 4.1.: Different Definitions of t-Visibility in Comparison in a (3,2,1) Quorum System

4.3.2. Ordering Violations

Wada et al. [98] propose to measure ordering via the client-centric ordering models MRC, RYWC and MWC. In their work, though, these metrics are binary – either fulfilled or not. We propose to extend this by using the likelihood of a violation of MRC, RYWC and MWC as ordering metrics[8].

The probability of violations for each ordering model is reproducible if the exact same workload can be recreated. Depending on the implementation, though, it may also be reproducible in a workload-independent measurement: For instance, in the case of MRC the probability of violation can be 0% if sticky sessions and suitable mechanisms for failure handling are used[9]. All three metrics are continuous and as fine-grained as possible for ordering metrics. They are meaningful to application developers who can use the information to efficiently handle inconsistencies at the application level. Storage providers might use these metrics to express consistency guarantees within a SLA.

Instead of the probability of violations, it would be even more precise if said probability was reported as a function of the duration since the last update. This becomes intuitive when

---

[8]The same can be done for WFRC, but actual measurements from a client perspective can be difficult as some insight into the storage system is required.

[9]In sticky sessions, all requests by a client are routed to the same replica. If this replica fails, the system needs to wait until all other replicas are up-to-date before routing the respective clients to a new replica. This is also often implemented as session consistency, where the guarantees only hold for the duration of a session. In that case, the failure handling need not be considered as a new session is started if a replica fails.

considering MRC in two extreme situations: In the first scenario, the last update was just one nanosecond ago. So, when reading any replica but the replica where the update originated, chances are that MRC will be violated. In a second scenario, the last update occurred several weeks ago. Now, the probability of violating MRC is zero. The probability values of an ordering violation obviously depend on the duration since the last update. Still, from an application developer's perspective, it will typically not be known *when* the last update was issued. So, while reporting the probability as a function of time may be more precise, it is also less meaningful to application developers. We, therefore, choose to report the aggregated value without a reference to the time interval since the last update.

4.4. Conclusion and Discussion

In this chapter, we started by defining criteria and requirements for consistency metrics – namely *reproducibility* (repeating a measurement should yield the same results), *high resolution* (measurements should be able to detect small as well as large consistency deviations), *fine granularity* (measurements should only analyze one attribute at a time), *meaningfulness* (measurement results should be meaningful to either or both storage providers and users).

Next, we discussed different data-centric metrics based on these criteria and identified t-Visibility, k-Staleness and Ordering Violations as "good" metrics, while Consistency Anomalies as well as Atomicity, Regularity and Safeness each violate at least one requirement. Finally, we did the same from a client perspective and identified client-centric t-Visibility and k-Staleness as well as client-centric Ordering Violations as valid metrics. Table 4.1 gives an overview of all valid metrics which we will use for the remainder of this thesis.

There is a general problem with all kinds of ordering metrics: While staleness can be measured entirely workload-independent[10], ordering highly depends on the workload. For instance, from a client perspective a workload could be such that the interval between requests is larger than the maximum client-centric t-Visibility. In that case, no violations of MRC or RYWC will ever be seen by the client. On the other hand, in a scenario where a client always first issues a write request followed by a read on the same key, the probability of RYWC violations mainly depends on the length of time between those operations. If t-Visibility is a constant of five seconds and this interval is four seconds, there will be 100% RYWC violations. If this interval is six seconds, there will be 0% RYWC violations.

It gets even more complicated in the face of failures: If, for example, a read request fails, there are two possible outcomes. Either the client will receive an error message and read

---

[10]Unless the system is overloaded with resource saturation levels close to 100%, staleness mainly depends on the time necessary to forward updates between replicas and the time needed to process these requests. If the system is overloaded, no general statement is possible as the system behavior then entirely depends on prioritization of processes. The same system configuration may even behave differently when deployed on different hardware or operating systems.

Metric	Staleness	Ordering	Perspective	Description
t-Visibility	X	-	Provider	Distribution function of data-centric inconsistency windows
k-Staleness	X	-	Provider	Distribution function of data-centric version lag
Ordering Violations	(X)	X	Provider	Violations per time or likelihood of violation of next stronger consistency model
t-Visibility	X	-	Client	Distribution function of client-centric inconsistency windows
k-Staleness	X	-	Client	Distribution function of client-observable version lag
Violations of MRC	-	X	Client	Probability of violation of MRC during reads
Violations of MWC	-	X	Client	Probability of violation of MWC for two consecutive writes
Violations of RYWC	-	X	Client	Probability of violation of RYWC during reads following a write

Table 4.1.: Overview of Consistency Metrics Fulfilling all Requirements

again right away or he will encounter a timeout much later. In the first case, the rate of requests during failures will actually increase while in the second case the rate of requests will in fact decrease. Both cases can have a large impact on consistency measurements in the presence of failures. Generally speaking, we can, hence, say that ordering cannot be measured workload-independent and that measurements for one workload may have little meaning or implication for another workload.

5. Modeling and Simulation of Consistency Behavior

Our objective for this chapter is a model to assess and compare the consistency behavior of arbitrary eventually consistent storage systems and their configurations, which does not require expensive experimental setup costs, but uses well-defined metrics and simulations to predict consistency behavior.

We start in section 5.1 by defining assumptions our modeling and simulation approach needs to make. Next, we present our model, comprising the following sub-models: The basic system model (section 5.2.1), the interaction model (section 5.2.2) and the failure model (section 5.2.3). Based on this model, two distinct simulation approaches are possible: either calculating convolutions which guarantee high precision results with limited output metrics and high computational effort (section 5.3.1) or Monte Carlo simulations (section 5.3.2), which offer approximations with less computational effort and which support all consistency metrics from chapter 4. We also show how the necessary simulation input data can be obtained, see section 5.3.3. Finally, we present a conclusion (section 5.4).

5.1. Assumptions

Our model assumes replication to be the main method for ensuring availability and scalability of the data store. To this end, the following additional assumptions are made.

1. *No byzantine failures*: We focus on modeling and simulating the result of the particular storage system's trade-off decision on the issue of latency versus consistency as well as availability versus consistency [45, 2], assuming that replicas will behave as intended (e.g., return the latest locally known version and not some random value). Crash-stop failures and crash-recover failures are supported (see section 5.2.3).

2. *No side effects*: Machines running the storage system in question or machines responsible for collecting our model's input data will not be affected in their performance by external effects, e.g., other software running on that machine. The same is true for the network connection between any two machines. Of course, the same holds for every kind of system benchmark. Hence, this assumption can be reduced to the requirement that collected simulation input data accurately reflects reality. For example, if we measure round trip times between two servers and always see a delay of 500ms in our

results, we assume that this is representative, i.e., that 500ms delay is accurate most of the time. This assumption is important as companies like Google are well known to run several different systems on the same machine. For obvious reasons, a storage system will show different behavior when, e.g., a MapReduce job is running on the same machine compared to when there is no other system running. This assumption does not preclude the simulation of storage systems running on a shared host (e.g., on a virtual machine in the cloud). Still, it requires that the parallel workload during the measurement of the input data is comparable to the parallel workload in the situation which shall be simulated.

3. *Only deterministic protocols for update propagations*: A request originating in a particular node will always be propagated in a deterministic way, i.e., at deploy time it is known which node will send its updates to which other node. It is acceptable that a particular node may have more than one node to which it will send its updates with a certain probability as long as this set of nodes and the corresponding probabilities are known at deploy time. This will usually be the case, e.g., for typical update propagation schemes like quorum or master-slave systems.

4. *Updates only execute based on update requests*: Systems often include specific mechanisms that change state during reads (e.g., read repair) or during periodic reconciliation. These mechanisms affect consistency behavior but are hard to include in a general model as it is not easily possible to determine when and where they are triggered. Furthermore, they are very system-specific. Therefore, we do not consider these mechanisms now and leave them to future extensions of our approach.

Apart from these assumptions our model is applicable to any kind of system which handles distributed state.

5.2. Model

Our model comprises three distinct parts which we describe in the following. The basic system model (section 5.2.1) can be used independently, while both the interaction model (section 5.2.2) and the failure model (section 5.2.3) are built on top of it.

5.2.1. Basic System Model

A network of interconnected replica servers can be described as a graph $G = (V, E)$ where the vertices $V(G)$ correspond to servers and the edges $E(G)$ describe the physical connections between those servers.

Sending data along a particular edge takes different amounts of time depending among others on the amount of data and the available bandwidth between the two vertices. We add these time differences as weights on the edges. In contrast to typical graph theory examples, though, our weights may vary over time and depend on a number of parameters. To reflect this, we use a family of probability density functions as edge weights. $L_{ij}(s)$ describes the probability distribution for one One-Way Data Transfer Time (ODTT) when sending data size s from vertex i to j. Specifically, $L_{ij}(s)$ is not required to be identical to $L_{ji}(s)$, though it is often likely to be so. Note, that ODTT is the time necessary to send data from A to B without any acknowledgments or response messages above the TCP layer.

Comparable to the edge weights, there is also something similar for the vertices: Requests are not only delayed when traveling over the network but also within a node as it takes some time to flush data to disk and to handle internal application logic. In geo-distributed deployments, these values will often be very small compared to $L_{ij}(s)$ values and can in those cases be neglected. We still include them in our model as they can have a large influence in single site deployments. Reads and updates both incur processing time overheads which depend on the available physical resources per node as well as the data size. We denote the respective families of probability density functions as $R_i(s)$ for reads and $W_i(s)$ for writes.

5.2.2. Interaction Model

While the basic system model from section 5.2.1 describes a system deployment, a storage system typically serves the purpose to be accessible from the outside. Depending on load balancer strategies or general policies, requests are routed to different replicas. Often, concurrent requests to the same key will originally be handled by different nodes. We categorize requests as either an update or a read operation as both may be handled entirely different. For example, in Yahoo's storage system PNUTS (Sherpa) [32] all update requests are processed at a master replica and then forwarded to the slaves using a system called Yahoo! Messaging Bus. Reads in contrast can be sent to any replica depending on whether the client allows eventually consistent reads or not.

To reflect these kinds of interaction in our basic system model, there is an arbitrary number of directed subgraphs $G_i = (V, E)$ for each vertex x_i which describe the update propagation path for the required set of replicas, i.e., who forwards updates to whom for all update requests originating in vertex x_i. We call those replication graphs. Furthermore, there may be an arbitrary number of directed subgraphs per vertex describing which replicas will be read by whom in which order upon a read request. We call those read graphs. Neither replication graphs nor read graphs need to reach all vertices (while replication graphs typically will and should reach all vertices, read graphs usually will only access a small subset). Figure 5.1

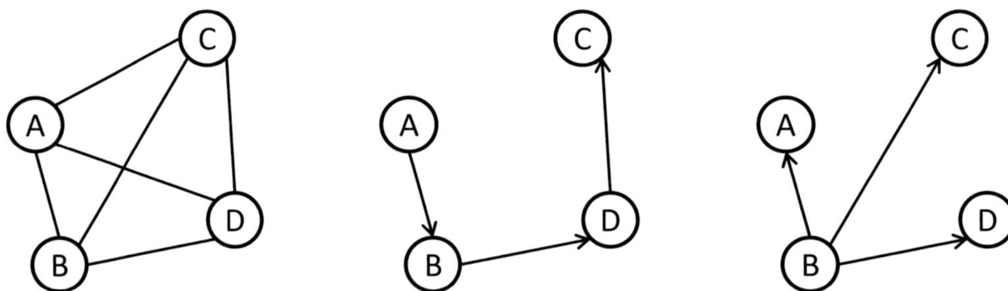

Figure 5.1.: Example for Replication and Read Graphs: The Set of Interconnected Replicas on the Left, a Possible Replication Graph for A (in the Middle), a Possible Read Graph for B (on the Right).

shows an example of a system graph and what its replication and read graphs might look like.

Each replication or read graph has not only a start vertex but also a probability value describing the likelihood of a write (or read respectively) request using that particular graph. We call those values p_i^W for replication graphs and p_i^R for read graphs. Probability values depend on load balancing strategies as well as geographical distribution of application workload and replicas.

Since update propagation and reads may happen synchronously, asynchronously or as part of a quorum, this needs to be considered within the interaction model. For this purpose, an edge of a replication or read graph is always part of a synchronicity group which belongs to the start vertex of that particular edge and has one of the three types named above: synchronous, asynchronous and quorum. In the latter case, it also includes information on the number of edges necessary to return success within that synchronicity group. As the name states, synchronicity groups may contain arbitrary numbers of edges. Based on this, it is possible to model all kinds of replication schemes ranging from master-slave setups to quorum systems and any possible combinations of those two.

5.2.3. Failure Model

There are two types of non-byzantine failures (see section 2.5): Crash-stop failures where a component becomes permanently unavailable (at least regarding a near time horizon) and crash-recover failures where a component becomes unavailable for a limited period of time.

We consider both types of failures in our model by assigning a set of unavailability intervals to each vertex and edge as additional weights. Sets may be empty and crash-stop failures can be modeled by setting the end value of the specific interval to infinity.

Correlated and/or catastrophic failures can be modeled by assigning appropriately correlated failure intervals to the respective components.

5.3. Simulation

There are two possible ways to simulate consistency behavior using our model, either via calculating convolutions or via a Monte Carlo simulation. The first approach offers the highest precision but is very compute-intensive, cannot consider failures and is limited to simulating data-centric t-Visibility. Monte Carlo simulations, in contrast, also allow to simulate failures as well as client-centric behavior and the compute effort is directly proportional to the level of precision required.

In the following, we first describe the simulation approach of using convolutions before continuing with Monte Carlo simulations.

5.3.1. Calculating Convolutions

When calculating convolutions, only data-centric t-Visibility can be calculated. Hence, the question of "how soon is eventual" essentially translates directly to "how long does it take to traverse the entire replication graph" for data-centric consistency.

For simulation purposes, we need to consider a replication graph as a tree with the originating vertex as the root node. The distribution of inconsistency windows can then be calculated as the convolution of all $L_{ij}(s)$ and $W_i(s)$ using different operators. The easiest to implement, though not very efficient, algorithm is to calculate the convolutions using the add operator along every path from root node to all leaves, first. In a second step, we can then calculate the convolution of all these results from step 1 using the max operator. In a third step, the results of step two for all replication paths are aggregated with the respective p_i^W of the root node as weights. The result of step three, then describes the distribution of data-centric t-Visibility for the analyzed configuration of the distributed storage system.

For systems without dirty reads, the result needs some additional calculation: The latency distribution can be calculated just like we did for the inconsistency window above. The difference is that not all paths from root to leaves are used, instead all synchronous paths from the root towards the leaves are considered. A synchronous path is a path where all edges are synchronous (to consider quorums is difficult if not impossible in this simple algorithm). It ends with a leaf or the vertex before an asynchronous edge – depending on which comes first. Finally, we can determine the difference between the observed inconsistency window and the latency distribution by calculating the convolution of both distributions using a subtract operator.

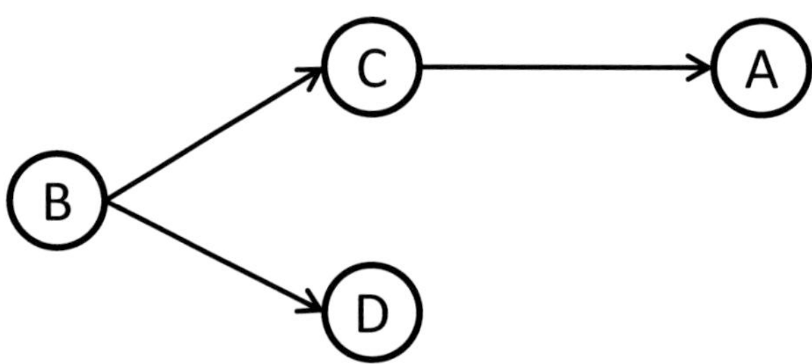

Figure 5.2.: Sample Replication Graph

For example, figure 5.2 shows a replication graph for write requests originating in vertex B. In the first step, we would then calculate the convolution of

1. $W_B(s)$, $L_{BC}(s)$, $W_C(s)$, $L_{CA}(s)$ and $W_A(s)$ using the add operator for every data size s.

2. $W_B(s)$, $L_{BD}(s)$ and $W_D(s)$ using the add operator for every data size s.

In the second step, we calculate the convolution of the two results from the first step using the max operator.

For reasons of legibility, we omit the formulas for calculating convolutions using different operators and present this approach in a more informal manner. Necessary formulas can be found in any statistics book or even on the Internet (e.g., [86]).

5.3.2. Monte Carlo Simulation

A Monte Carlo simulation requires a small extension of the model described above which then also allows client-centric consistency simulation. One or more entities external to the system graph, the clients, issue requests of a specific type (read or write) at a specific start time. Furthermore, as concurrent updates can be simulated, it is necessary to specify a conflict resolution strategy. Possible strategies are

- Last write wins: Updates are applied strictly in the order that they arrive at the respective replica. Hence, replicas may have different values and may only converge upon another isolated write[1].

- Write set: This approach is similar to the understanding of consistency in GFS [44] where a replica is consistent if it contains all updates independent of their order. Essentially, writes are added to a set or appended to a log.

---

[1] Apache Cassandra (cassandra.apache.org) uses a slightly different last write wins strategy where clients timestamp their requests and these timestamps are used by Cassandra to determine which update was "last".

- Return competing writes: The system uses mechanisms like vector clocks to identify concurrent updates and returns all conflicting values upon a read. The next write by the same client is expected to resolve the conflict if no further writes occurred in between. This approach is, e.g., taken in Amazon's Dynamo [37].

We propose to simulate the consistency behavior in three phases, the first two are identical for all strategies. The benefit of separating simulation data generation and evaluation is that a simulated request log could, at least theoretically, be analyzed for several conflict resolution strategies. Furthermore, no limitations need to be made on the creation order of requests.

As a side effect, the Monte Carlo simulation can also produce latency and availability predictions[2].

Phase 1 A large number of simulated requests is created. For each request, a replication or read graph is chosen based on the request type (read/write) and the appropriate values p_i^W and p_i^R. The graph is then traversed to identify when processing starts and ends in which node. For each start or end timestamp, an event is created.

During event generation, failures are considered by failing all requests that would incur an error somewhere along their synchronous subgraph and delaying all asynchronous parts until all respective components are available again. The difficult part is here, that delays due to temporary failures influence the evaluation of quorum synchronicity groups. We do not include a detailed algorithm listing here for reasons of legibility but we intend to publish our simulation tool as open source. More details can also be found in chapter 7

Finally, events are written into a simulated log containing start and end events for individual writes and reads in vertices, operation starts, ends or fails as well as the list of vertices participating in a read graph result.

Phase 2 This phase checks for data-centric consistency by first grouping all events within the log by their (unique) operation id and then calculating the difference in time between the first and the last timestamp as data-centric inconsistency window (t-Visibility[3]). The output of this phase is, hence, the distribution of data-centric inconsistency windows, latencies and the error rate. Results are reported both per replication graph and global (i.e., the aggregation of all replication graphs).

---

[2]This is implemented in our simulation tool but we will not evaluate it as the focus of this work is the consistency assessment. Simulating response times and availability levels is beyond the scope of this thesis.

[3]For t-Visibility without Dirty Reads, the algorithm does not need to change. Only different start events need to be used. In our implementation this is supported without changes to the code.

Phase 3   The third phase checks for client-centric consistency. For this purpose, every simulated read request has to be analyzed: Based on the strategy specified above[4], the list of vertices participating in the results and the respective read start timestamps as well as the respective write end timestamps in these vertices, our simulation tool identifies the writes contained in the response of that read request (or the result of the operation depending on the strategy). Comparing this information to the operation end timestamps of all writes (commit timestamps) yields whether the read was stale.

Furthermore, when we set this result in relation to a) all write operation end timestamps by the same client and b) all previous reads by the same client, we can easily determine whether MRC or RYWC were violated.

Using the list of reads and the respectively contained writes, we can then calculate client-centric t-Visibility (in this case: timestamp of the last read without a specific write minus the timestamp of the operation end or start).

Currently, this phase logs for each read operation whether results were stale and whether MRC or RYWC were violated. It also reports for each write the commit timestamp and the last time a client saw a read results not containing this specific write. Additional evaluation could be added if necessary[5]. Based on this information, a simple spreadsheet analysis can determine the probability of MRC and RYWC violations as well as the client-centric t-Visibility.

5.3.3. Simulation Input Data

Running a simulation requires knowledge of all parameters described in sections 5.2.1, 5.2.2 and 5.2.3. We now discuss briefly how these values can be measured in a real-world distributed storage system.

One-way Data Transfer Times   ODTT values are hard to determine accurately due to clock synchronisation issues. Essentially, there are two different ways: either measuring ODTT values directly, thus, relying on the precision of the underlying clock synchronisation protocol or accurately measuring Round Trip Time (RTT). For our purposes an RTT value comprises the establishment of a connection, the transfer of data from A to B as well as, after the first transfer completes, the data transfer from B to A using the same connection. In contrast, an ODTT value comprises the time necessary for creating a connection and the data transfer from A to B or only the data transfer if connections are reused. In a perfect world,

---

[4]*Last write wins*, *Write set* or *Return competing writes*. We have currently only implemented the *Write set* strategy as this is the most generic strategy which the other two strategies build upon. Furthermore, the other two strategies are actually groups of strategies and often system-dependent.

[5]Based on the output of phase 1, the algorithms of Anderson et al. [6] and Golab et al. [46] could be used to also calculate consistency results in terms of their proposed consistency metrics if desired.

ODTT values would be exactly half the RTT. But since there is an overhead to establish the connection, fill the first TCP buffer etc., half the RTT is a lower bound for our desired ODTT values. On the other end, there is always some time necessary to return the message to the sender. So, ODTT will always be less than RTT. This leads to something like ODTT $=$ $k * RTT$ with $k \in (0.5; 1)$. We believe, that concrete values for k mainly depend on the number of concurrent connections, something we have also seen in experiments. It should be mentioned, though, that we have never seen k values of 0.5 in actual measurements. In future work we want to address the question of choosing correct values for k, using both work from the clock synchronisation community as well as network protocol research as input. For this reason, we currently measure ODTT values directly, accepting NTP [6] accuracy.

ODTT values are not only affected by the available bandwidth between two nodes but also by the communication middleware used. It is, therefor, necessary to use the same communication middleware for the measurement of ODTT values that the simulated storage system uses. For example, in the case of Apache Cassandra this would be Thrift[7]. As we have seen when using our own simple communication middleware system (which was specifically *not* designed for performance), ODTT values may be in entirely different dimensions (in this case a factor of 10 compared to ping).

Processing Times In theory, $W_i(s)$ and $R_i(s)$ should be relatively easy to determine, e.g., by mining server-side logs. If access to the source code is not possible, external tools like Wireshark[8] could be used to determine the distribution of durations between receiving a request and responding (in that case, though, it is necessary to somehow correlate inbound and outbound communication). These values are likely to be affected by other programs running on the same machine. In practice, though, we have encountered inaccuracies as processing times heavily vary with the system load and, thus, have slightly different values also depending on replication schemes (if node A forwards requests to a higher number of nodes than node B, then A will typically have a slightly higher system load and larger $W_i(s)$ values).

For geo-distributed replication, values are typically very small in relation to ODTT so that inaccuracies can be neglected. It is even possible to use a constant value instead of a distribution family to reduce calculation effort during simulations.

For single site deployments, processing times have a higher impact. We believe that the results for S3 of [17] are mainly caused by artificially induced processing overheads. Here, processing times limit the precision of the simulation results.

---

[6]ntp.org
[7]thrift.apache.org
[8]wireshark.org

We currently use logging to identify an approximate distribution. Still, there is a lot of room for improvements in obtaining processing time values.

Request Probabilities p_i^W and p_i^R can again be determined using server-side operation logs. It is, for example, possible to count read and write requests per replica and divide them by the sum of all read or write requests in the system, respectively. Another alternative is prior knowledge on system setup (e.g., for master-slave systems or globally distributed deployments) or direct access to the load balancer which is used. In the latter case, the respective load balancing strategy can be identified.

5.4. Conclusion

In this part, we started with a general discussion of our Consistency Benchmarking approach using both simulation and system benchmarking. After discussing consistency metrics in chapter 4, we introduced within this chapter a new approach for modeling and simulating the consistency behavior of distributed storage systems. Based on graph theory, our modeling and simulation approach comprises the basic system model (section 5.2.1), the interaction model (section 5.2.2) and the failure model (section 5.2.3). Building on this model, our approach includes two simulation modes: either calculating convolutions which guarantee high precision results with limited output metrics and high computational effort (section 5.3.1) or Monte Carlo simulations (section 5.3.2), which offer approximations with less computational effort and which support all consistency metrics from chapter 4. Afterwards, we discussed how the necessary simulation input data can be obtained and which problems can occur (section 5.3.3).

Our approach does not require expensive setups, and can be applied to diverse storage systems. The flexibility of our model, though, comes with a set of assumptions (section 5.1). Some of these could be relaxed or even completely avoided in future work.

6. System Benchmarking for Consistency Behavior

In this chapter, we present system benchmarking approaches which can be used to determine consistency behavior of distributed storage systems experimentally. This can either be done from a provider perspective for data-centric consistency behavior or from a client perspective – via black box testing – for client-centric consistency behavior. All these system benchmarking approaches can be used independently or as a second phase to verify findings obtained via simulation (see chapter 5).

We start with the discussion of challenges in section 6.1. Based on the metrics from chapter 4, we then describe how data-centric (section 6.2) and client-centric (section 6.3) consistency metrics can be measured in experiments.

This chapter includes and is based on material previously published in MW4SOC 2011 [17], NETYS 2013 [15], TPCTC 2013 [19] and IC2E 2014 [18].

6.1. Challenges

Apart from choosing appropriate metrics fulfilling the requirements outlined in chapter 4, a system benchmarking approach should in general, but specifically for consistency behavior, consider the following challenges:

Resolution A system benchmarking and measurement approach should not only use a metric with sufficiently high resolution (see chapter 4), but also needs to be able to make "use" of that resolution. This means that measurements should be done in a way that even close-by output values can be distinguished. For instance, in the case of a time-based metric, the sample rate in measurements per time should be as high as possible[1].

Wide Applicability A measurement approach should not be limited to a specific system. Instead, in the interest of comparability of results, it should be able to cover a broad range of systems. Hence, such a system benchmarking approach should use as little features of the storage system under examination as possible since the applicability of the system benchmark will be limited to all storage systems offering the respective set of features.

---

[1]For reasons of efficiency, though, it should be only as high as necessary.

Reproducibility   When repeating a system benchmark, the measurement component should produce similar results under the assumption that the storage system behaves comparably.

Accuracy   Measurements always include measurement errors – these should be small in relation to the values measured.

Ability to Analyze Influence Factors   Consistency is not an isolated property; it depends, among others, on the consistency versus latency and consistency versus availability trade-offs (see section 2.3), as well as on factors like replica placement and replication strategies. System benchmarks for consistency should, hence, be able to study the effects of those influence factors; system benchmarks should make as little assumptions as possible on system setup so as not to preclude the study of certain influence factors.

While there are obviously limitations regarding the degree to which these challenges are addressed, a comprehensive system benchmark for consistency behavior should strive to consider them as far as possible.

6.2. Data-centric Consistency

Running system benchmarks for data-centric consistency behavior requires access to either sufficiently detailed operation and commit logs or to the storage system's code to implement adequate logging functionality. A log should for each operation contain information on the operation identifier, the issuing client, the type of operation and its parameter and result list, as well as the timestamps describing when this operation was executed in which replica. This is necessary to determine among others the commit order of operations. Furthermore, a workload needs to be run against the storage system.

Data-centric t-Visibility can then be calculated as the difference in time between writing the last replica and either the start of the operation (t-Visibility with Dirty Reads) or the commit timestamp (t-Visibility without Dirty Reads).

Ordering violations can be determined by first analyzing the commit order per replica:

- If this order is identical for all replicas, then the system either fulfills LIN (if all reads also returned the result of the latest commited write) or SC (in all other cases). If only SC is fulfilled, then the number of violating reads needs to be counted. Afterwards, it can either be divided by the total number of reads (resulting in the likelihood of violation) or by the test duration as the violation rate.

- If not, the causal order of operations needs to be determined to check whether the system shows CC or EC behavior. If the individual replicas's operation logs have a causal order, then CC is fulfilled and the number of write requests where SC was violated needs to be counted. This number of violations can then again be divided by either the test duration or the total number of writes. If SC was not fulfilled, the number of violations needs to be counted and then divided by either the total number of all requests or the test duration.

This simple algorithm determines the data-centric ordering[2] behavior of a storage system.

6.3. Client-centric Consistency

System benchmarking for client-centric consistency is, in contrast to measurements of data-centric consistency, possible for every kind of storage system or service as it requires only black box access to the storage system; no additional logging functionality is required since only the access operations offered by the storage system (read and write operations) are used. In the absence of detailed logs, system benchmarking for client-centric consistency can even be used to approximate data-centric consistency behavior.

For system benchmarking of client-centric consistency, there are two competing effects: Accuracy requires having measurement clients close to the replicas as latencies increase the uncertainty level of the measurement results. Hence, an optimal solution would be to use as many measurement clients as possible, preferably co-located with the replica servers.

On the other hand, having more than one measurement client results in clock synchronization issues as physical clocks are always skewed. While clock synchronization algorithms like the Network Time Protocol (NTP)[3] help to reduce the skew in clocks, they still cannot prevent that single clocks may deviate faster from the correct time than the algorithm can offset the error. The chance of this happening obviously increases with the number of measurement clients used and skewed clocks clearly affect the accuracy of client-centric consistency measurement results. Hence, from a clock synchronization perspective, accuracy is maximized when using just one measurement client only.

In practice, using an adequate number of measurement clients while carefully observing results of individual clients is a dominant strategy. This way, measurement clients with heavily skewed clocks can be detected and their output be excluded from the aggregated results. What an "adequate" number of measurement clients is, depends on the consistency metric of interest, the replication factor, and the load balancing strategy. In the following, we discuss how each of the client-centric consistency metrics from section 4.3 can be measured experimentally.

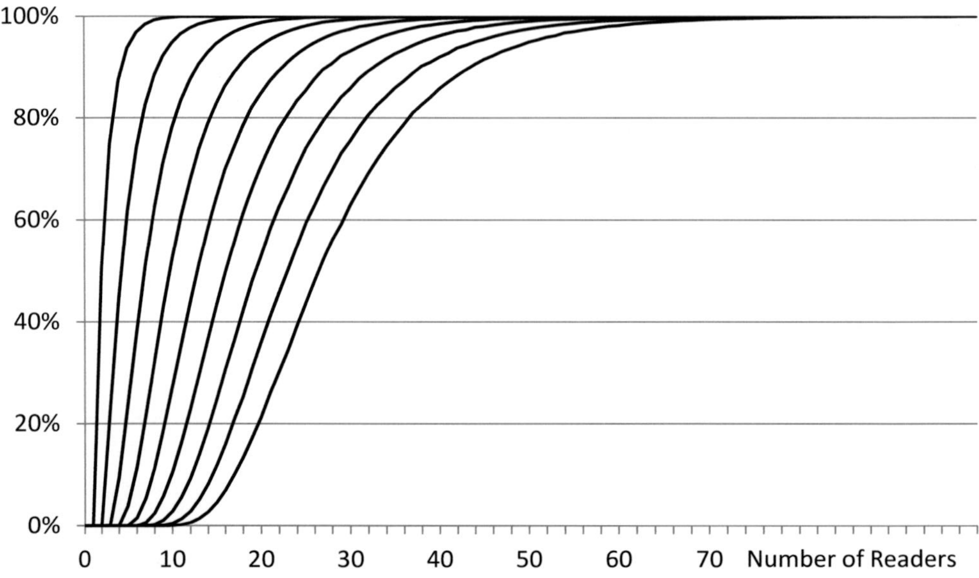

Figure 6.1.: Probabilities of Reaching all Replicas for Different Replication Factors as a Function of the Number of Readers

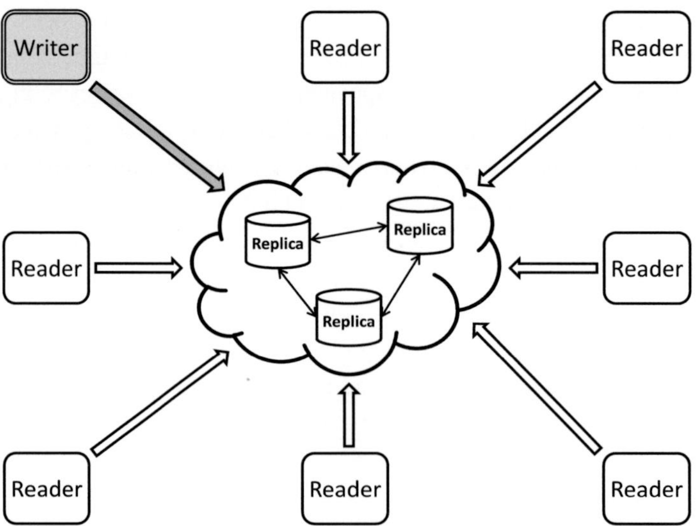

Figure 6.2.: System Benchmarking Setup for Staleness Measurements of Storage Systems with Load Balancer

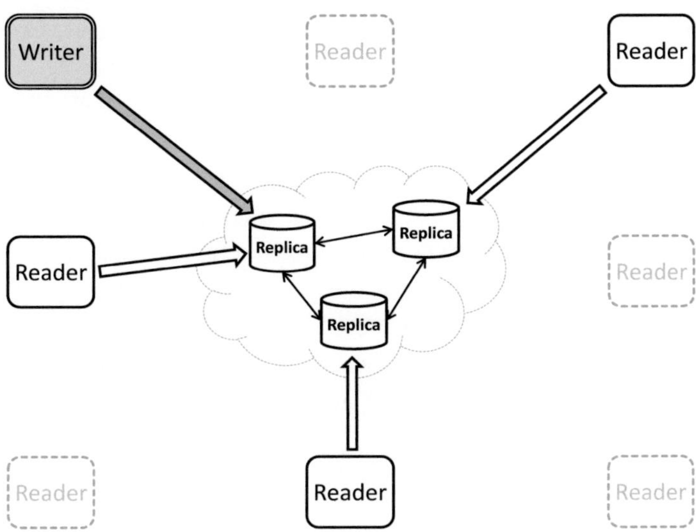

Figure 6.3.: System Benchmarking Setup for Staleness Measurements of Storage Systems with Direct Replica Access

6.3.1. t-Visibility and k-Staleness

As already discussed, staleness measurements require a number of geographically distributed measurement clients which are located as close as possible to the replica servers; these include at least one writer and a number of readers[4]. We have to distinguish two classes of systems: In the first category, requests are always directed to the load balancer which in turn forwards them to one or more replicas. So, access to the replicas is only via the load balancer; this is typically the case for cloud storage services. In the second category, there will usually be a load balancer, too. Still, the individual endpoints of the replica servers are known so that requests cannot only be directed to the load balancer but also to a specific replica. Self-hosted NoSQL systems normally fall in this category. Often, systems from the first group, especially cloud storage services, tend to show even higher degrees of transparency or uncertainty in that they do not even promote the replication factor used.

For staleness measurements, the test setup for both classes of systems is different:

Load Balancer-based Access Load Balancers often use strategies where requests are either routed to the geographically closest replica (especially in the case of geographically distributed storage systems) or using round-robin routing. Based on this strategy

---

[2] Violations of LIN obviously considers also staleness.

[3] ntp.org

[4] We discuss their precise roles later.

and the (potentially estimated) replication factor, we can calculate the probability of reading all replicas if n readers issue a read request at the same time. For example, in a scenario with round-robin routing and triple replication, there is a probability of 83% of reaching all replicas when using seven readers. For eight readers, this is about 88%, for nine readers 93% and so on. Based on the accuracy requirements of the measurements, an adequate number of readers should be chosen. To be on the safe side, we propose to use twelve readers for the scenario in our example. Figure 6.1 shows the probabilities of reaching all replicas as a function of the number of readers. Each curve represents a different replication factor, starting with two on the left up to 10 on the right. Figure 6.2 shows an exemplary setup.

Direct Replica Access If replicas can be accessed directly, the test setup is less probabilistic. Here, we just need one reader per replica which suffices to achieve a 100% probability of reaching all replicas when all readers issue their read request at the same time. Obviously, the replication factor is also known. If direct access to replicas is available, it should be used as it both reduces cost as well as increases accuracy of staleness measurements. Figure 6.3 shows in an exemplary setup how the number of readers can be reduced compared to the setup in figure 6.2.

When the adequate number of readers has been identified, these have to be deployed as close as possible to the replica servers. So, if the data store uses geographic replication, then the readers also need to be distributed.

During a system benchmark, the two roles – reader and writer – have different responsibilities: The writer periodically issues an update request containing a version number and the current timestamp to the distributed storage system. The interval between writes should be larger than the expected maximum t-Visibility. If not the system benchmark has to be repeated. At the same time, each reader continuously issues read requests to the storage system and logs which version and timestamp combination was read at which local timestamp.

Based on the logs of all readers, t-Visibility values can easily be determined – either as a probability density function showing the probability of a particular inconsistency window length, or as a function showing the probability of reading fresh versus stale values over time, thus, considering the results of all read operations instead of only those with maximum staleness values.

As already mentioned in chapter 4, k-Staleness values can be measured as a byproduct of t-Visibility measurements. In our case, the logs also include the version number so that k-Staleness can be calculated – either as a function showing k-Staleness development over time, or as the probability of reading a datum which is a number of n versions lagging behind.

6.3.2. Violations of Monotonic Read Consistency

Violations of MRC can often be measured as a byproduct of the staleness measurements. This is possible when the storage system was only accessed via the load balancer, because MRC guarantees heavily depend on the load balancer strategy used. E.g., using sticky sessions guarantees MRC and routing requests to the closest replica also tends to assure that MRC is preserved for most requests. Alternatively, it is possible to use a more complex workload with several writers or to run an actual application workload where each machine is both a reader and a writer. Afterwards, an offline analysis can determine (based on logs) the likelihood of MRC violations.

When using more than one writer, the application needs to assert that a total order of updates can still be established as the definition of MRC requires reading versions that are at least as new as all versions that have already been seen. This is necessary to determine whether a value that was read violates MRC or not. In a setup with more than one writer, there are several possible outcomes of two subsequent reads which return values A (first read) and B (second read):

- A and B are identical. Reading the same version twice does not violate MRC.

- A and B are not identical. Reading a different version can be caused by three effects:

  - A is newer than B, hence, MRC is violated.

  - A and B are parallel branches so that neither is newer than the other. In this case, it depends on the exact definition of MRC. If A was – in the replica that we read from – overwritten by B even though it was a parallel branch, then MRC is – strictly spoken – not violated. In all other cases, the replica that we read from did apparently not know about version A, so that MRC was violated. For a system like Dynamo [37], where differing versions and the respective vector clocks will be returned during reads, these two cases can be distinguished easily. In all other systems, we propose to consider both cases as a violation of MRC since the content, that we had seen previously, was obviously not contained in the result due to the missing causal relationship.

  - A is older than B, hence, MRC is not violated.

In contrast to staleness measurements, clock synchronization is not an issue as only the causal relationships of operations are of interest. Only if global MRC guarantees shall be considered, is it necessary to synchronize the clocks of the measurement clients.

6.3.3. Violations of Read Your Writes Consistency

Like MRC measurements, RYWC measurements also depend on the load balancing strategy used. Depending on the likelihood of routing requests by the same client to the same replica for every request, the probability of RYWC violations changes. RYWC measurements, hence, need to access the storage system via the load balancer, too.

For measurements, a single machine writes a value into the storage system (via the load balancer) and directly starts to continuously read it afterwards and logs the time difference to the end of the update as well as whether it was possible to read the new value or not. If this is repeated a statistically significant number of times, then it is possible to calculate the probability distributions for violations of RYWC as a function of the duration since the last update during an offline analysis after the system benchmarking run. Of course, it is also possible to calculate the probability of violating RYWC independent of time.

Furthermore, it is also possible to run a more complex workload with several machines reading and writing from and to the data store at the same time. This can easily be done in parallel to MRC measurements. Still, the same limitations regarding causal relationships hold as in the case of MRC. The only difference to the discussion above is that value A was not read but instead written by the measurement client.

Clock synchronization again only matters if global RYWC shall be measured.

6.3.4. Violations of Monotonic Write Consistency

For MWC guarantees, time does not matter, e.g., it does not matter which value is returned right after two subsequent writes. Only the final serialization order is important. Therefore, we propose to have a single machine insert a value into the storage system and directly update it afterwards. After waiting for a sufficiently long period of time (all replicas need to synchronize), the same key is read again and the result is compared to the updated value. If this is repeated for a large number of keys, the probability distribution for violations of MWC can be calculated.

In practice, we propose to wait for at least the maximum t-Visibility value plus a safety margin. If time is not an issue, it will probably be safe to check the results a day later. If the time window chosen is too small, then MWC measurements will not report MWC behavior but rather staleness and/or RYWC levels.

6.3.5. Violations of Write Follows Read Consistency

So far, no system benchmarking approach exists for WFRC violations. This can be explained by the fact that a violation cannot be directly observed by a client. One approach could be to use the replica logs of the storage system to identify if and how often WFRC has been violated. This is, obviously, no longer compatible with the black box access which is one of the strengths of client-centric consistency measurements. Using that approach, WFRC could, for instance, not be measured for cloud storage services.

Another approach could rely on the fact that WFRC violations mainly cause the effect that a delayed update message of an older version replaces the update that was executed on an older replica. If, for example, a client reads version $n + 10$ and then issues an update which executes on a replica still at version n, then (depending on the storage system's implementation) either a delayed update message for version $n + 10$ may replace the client's update (which leads to a lost update) or a conflicting version will be created which needs to be reconciled at a later point in time. If neither effect becomes visible, it still does *not* imply that WFRC is guaranteed.

Finally, a third approach only works for storage systems which offer update operations beyond a Create-Read-Update-Delete (CRUD) interface. For example, a record append operation like in the Google File System [44] could be used, followed by an analysis of the update order within the file.

All in all, we believe that no standard mechanism for measuring WFRC violations can exist.

6.4. Conclusion

In this chapter, we have presented system benchmarking approaches for consistency behavior. We started with a discussion of challenges in system benchmarking of consistency behavior and continued with data-centric consistency measurements which can be done via mining of replica logs. For client-centric consistency measurements, we have presented an approach which can be used to measure t-Visibility, k-Staleness and MRC violations. We have also discussed how violations of the other three client-centric ordering models could be measured. All of the presented approaches should be able to address the challenges from section 6.1 as much as possible, when used sensibly.

Generally, there is a direct relationship between data-centric and client-centric consistency guarantees. This can be seen in the fact, that data-centric consistency measurements can be used to estimate client-centric behavior and vice versa.

Part III.

Application

This Part shall demonstrate the applicability of our approaches from Part II. For us, applicability covers three points of importance:

1. *Proof of Concept*

2. *Correctness*

3. *Relevance*

We believe that an approach is only helpful if it can actually be implemented in practice – we try to prove this point by describing our proof of concept implementations in chapter 7.

A new approach should also demonstrate that it is in some way "better" than existing ones (if there are any) and that it shows correct behavior, i.e., in our case measures or predicts correct results. As there are no or few comparable approaches, correctness can for our approaches either be shown by formal proof or in experiments. We chose to evaluate our approaches experimentally – see chapter 8.

Finally, we believe that any new approach should solve a relevant problem and clearly demonstrate what it is good for. For this purpose, we demonstrate, using an example, in chapter 9, how actual applications can handle inconsistencies leveraging knowledge on consistency behavior. We, then, describe how MRC and RYWC can be guaranteed within a middleware component running on the same machine(s) as the application logic. Finally, we show how the results of Consistency Benchmarking can help to both increase the efficiency of such an approach as well as to offer additional guarantees beyond MRC and RYWC.

7. Implementation

As a proof of concept, we have implemented each of our approaches presented in chapters 5 and 6. In this chapter, we introduce these proof of concept implementations starting with our modeling and simulation approach (section 7.1) before continuing with our system benchmarking approach (section 7.2).

This chapter contains material previously published in MW4SOC 2011 [17], TPCTC 2013 [19], and IC2E 2014 [18].

7.1. Modeling and Simulation

The prototype of our modeling and simulation approach as well as a data gathering tools for ODTT and RTT values have been implemented in Java 7. In this section, we briefly sketch out how our data gathering tools work before continuing to our simulation tools.

7.1.1. Data Gathering Tools

As already discussed in section 5.3.3, RTT can be measured without any negative influence from inaccuracies in clock synchronization. At the same time, RTT values cannot be directly used for simulations as ODTT values are necessary. To check the ratio between RTT and ODTT values, we implemented data gathering tools for both and used it to compare the respective results; RTT values were subject to NTP accuracy. Both tools are deployed on several distributed servers and communicate via a configurable communication middleware system.

For RTT measurements, the tool is started with the addresses of all servers as well as the desired data packet size as parameters. Each server then proceeds to randomly choose another server, create a new random data packet and send it to the target server. At the same time, each target server echoes any request it receives so that the original sender can measure the time necessary for sending a data packet over the network and reading it back. This happens until the tool is terminated; at that time, each server locally logs the observed RTT values grouped by the respective target servers. Each server is running both a sender and target thread.

For ODTT measurements, the RTT tool is changed in that the servers do not wait for an echo message but instead close the connection right after completing the transmission. Each data packet is assigned a unique ID and while the sender logs the start time for that ID, the receiving server logs the end time for the respective ID. Afterwards, an analysis tool merges the individual log files and outputs the measured ODTT values grouped by the combination of sender and target.

Calculated distributions of ODTT values (either directly measured or calculated as a fraction of RTT values) are then used as input for our simulation tools.

7.1.2. Simulation Tools

As already discussed in sections 5.3.1 and 5.3.2, there are two ways for simulating consistency: Either by calculating convolutions or by running a Monte Carlo simulation.

Calculating Convolutions

For calculating convolutions, we implemented a tool in Java 6 which takes two or three random distributions (based on discrete input values) and a configurable and arbitrarily extensible operator as parameters and outputs the convolution of those two distributions based on the respective operator. Output and input formats are identical so that the output of one calculation can be used as the input for the next one. This way, arbitrary replication paths can be calculated. Currently, we have implemented the following operators: add, subtract, multiply, maximum and minimum.

Our tool for calculating convolutions is extensible and easy to use. On the other hand, it underlies the general limitations of calculating convolutions which we already mentioned in section 5.3.1 and is not optimized for performance.

Monte Carlo Simulation

Our Java 7 implementation of Monte Carlo simulations is a rather complex tool. For ease of implementation, our tool deviates slightly from the general modeling and simulation approach presented in sections 5.2 and 5.3.2:

- We assume that distributions $L_{ij}(s)$ and $L_{ji}(s)$ are identical, i.e., sending data from A to B is as fast as sending data the other way around. This is frequently the case, especially for deployment in data centers. For situations, where one replica is running at an end user's home this is not feasible as in that case the available bandwidth for upstream and downstream will be different.

- Our implementation currently uses a single probability density function instead of a family of probability density functions depending on the parameter s for data size. This functionality could be added with very little effort but is currently not supported.

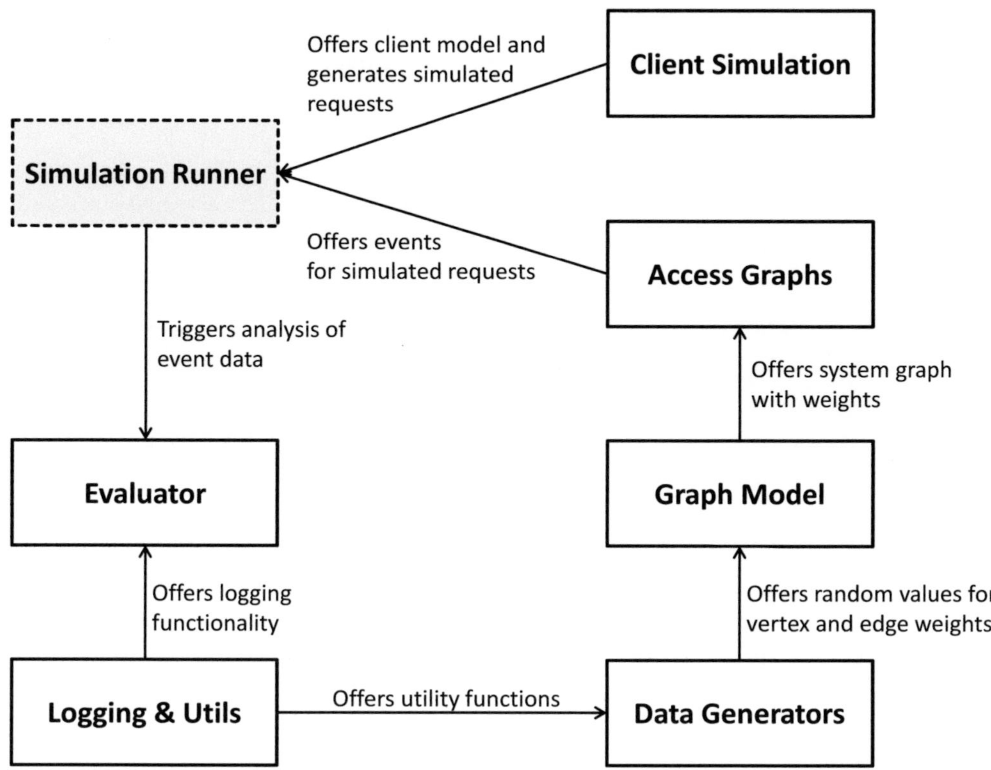

Figure 7.1.: Overview of Software Modules in the Monte Carlo Simulation Tool

- Our analysis module currently uses only the *Write Set* mechanism for conflict resolution in concurrent updates. Other mechanisms can be used by adding another analysis module or by extending the current one.

- In chapter 4, we discussed different staleness metrics for systems with or without dirty reads. Our current implementation uses the one with dirty reads in a hard-coded way. Changing this requires to switch the order of a few lines of code.

Our tool comprises seven main modules which are depicted in figure 7.1. In the following, we describe each of these modules.

Data Generators   The *Data Generators* module includes two extensible groups of classes: Delay generators implement a method `getRandomDelay()` which is used to draw random values for edge weights (ODTT values $L_{ij}(s)$) and vertex weights (processing times $W_i(s)$ and $R_i(s)$). Error generators, in contrast, implement a method `getUnavailablePeriods(long` `start, long end`) which randomly selects times of unavailability within the simulated time interval $[start; end]$ and returns this set of intervals. Currently, there are three generators each but additional ones can be added by extending an abstract class:

- Delay Generators:

    - `ConstantDelayGenerator` is parameterized with a fixed value and always returns this very same value as delay. This is useful when only a mean value but not variance is known.

    - `ExponentialDelayGenerator` is parameterized with a mean value and returns random values drawn from the corresponding exponential distribution.

    - `DiscreteDistributionDelayGenerator` is parameterized with a list of delay values typically measured experimentally. Upon request it randomly selects one of those values and returns it.

- Error Generators:

    - `NoErrorGenerator` returns an empty set of unavailability intervals and is used for simulations where no error shall occur.

    - `MTBFandMTTRErrorGenerator` is parameterized with MTBF and Mean Time To Repair (MTTR) values (including the corresponding variances) and randomly selects values according to the parameters.

    - `DiscretePeriodErrorGenerator` is parameterized with a set of intervals and returns this very same set. This is useful when either running simulations based on historic data or when rerunning simulations.

Graph Model The *Graph Model* module has exactly four classes which build the basic system graph, i.e., hold information which is shared by all replication and read paths.

The abstract class `AbstractComponent` holds information on a component identifier, a screen name as well as a reference to the respective error generator used. Its two extending classes `Vertex` and `Edge` hold references to the respective delay generators as well as to the edges of the vertex (class `Vertex`) and the two vertices of an edge (class `Edge`). Hence, our implementation uses doubly linked object references as in-memory graph representation which is useful for iterating over the graph.

Finally, the singleton `ComponentRegistry` references the graph itself and offers functionality to query and to manipulate it. It is, thus, the point of entry for all other modules.

Access Graphs The *Access Graphs* module comprises both a model to describe replication and read paths as well as the functionality to simulate a request using such a path, i.e., to

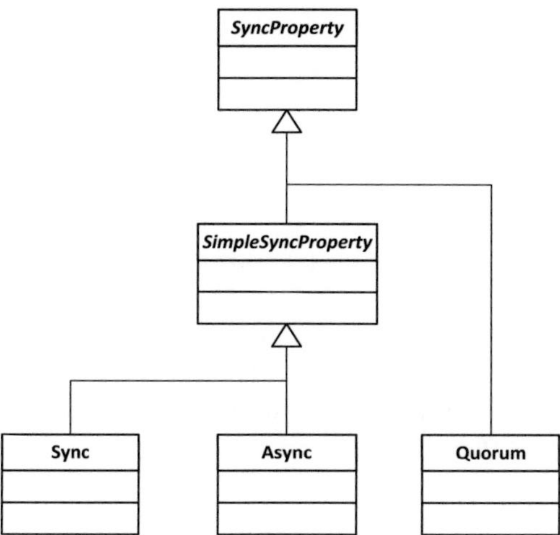

Figure 7.2.: UML Class Diagram of the Synchronicity Group Implementation

create all events. This is implemented by an abstract class `AccessGraph` and its two extending classes `ReadGraph` and `ReplicationGraph`. Most functionality for graph iteration is identical for both read and replication paths and is, therefore, already implemented within the abstract super class. The singleton `AccessGraphRegistry` holds references to all existing replication and read paths and serves as access point for other modules.

As discussed in section 5.2.2, synchronicity groups describe how edges are used – either synchronously or asynchronously. To also support quorums [94], our implementation uses a separate object hierarchy to determine which edges will actually be used synchronously or asynchronously. An abstract class `SyncProperty` defines a method `simulateAccess()` which takes an array of latency values as parameter (one for each edge within the group) and returns an array of `SimpleSyncProperty` instances one each correspoding to the respective edge (i.e., in the same order as the parameter values).

`SyncProperty` has two child classes `Quorum` and `SimpleSyncProperty`; the latter is abstract and extended by the classes `Sync` and `Async`. The classes `Sync`, `Async` and `Quorum` each implement the method originally defined in `SyncProperty`, so that `Sync` returns an array of `Sync` objects, `Async` returns an array of `Async` objects and `Quorum` returns a mixture of both depending on the parameters and the quorum setting for the respective synchronicity group.

Figure 7.2 shows a UML class diagram of this part of the *Access Graphs* module.

Client Simulation The *Client Simulation* module creates simulated requests according to predefined client behavior. For this purpose, there is an abstract class `AbstractClient` which defines abstract methods `generateReadStarts()` and `generateWriteStarts()`. Both methods take the start and end timestamp of the simulation period as parameters and return a list of start timestamps for simulated read and write requests respectively. Arbitrary implementations can be added beyond the two child classes which currently exist:

- `OperationLogClient` is parameterized with start timestamps from an actual operation log. This is useful for replaying a workload scenario with different configurations.

- `RandomizedClient` is a probabilistic implementation which is parameterized with the information on the desired number of reads and writes per second and randomly selects timestamps within the test interval to fulfill these requirements. Timestamp selection is based on a uniform distribution.

The `RequestScheduler` then randomly selects a replication/read path according to the preferences specified in the *Access Graphs* module and, during the actual Monte Carlo simulation, serves as an iterator over the set of simulated requests.

Simulation Runner   The *Simulation Runner* module is the core component of the Monte Carlo simulation phase: Based on an existing configuration from the modules *Graph Model* and *Access Graphs*, it triggers the request generation from the *Client Simulation* module and submits each of the simulated requests to the *Access Graphs* module which then determines the start and end timestamps for each vertex as well as the operation outcome. Finally, the *Simulation Runner* module triggers event analysis within the *Evaluator* module.

Evaluator   The *Evaluator* module is called with the list of all simulated events (operation start, end, or fail, as well as request start or end for all replicas) and analyses these events to determine the simulated consistency behavior. For this purpose, the current implementation[1] executes the following steps:

1. Group events by their operation ID and kind (read or write) and determine whether these requests were successful or failed.

2. Calculate the data-centric t-Visibility based on all write operations that were successful.

3. Calculate the distribution of read and write latencies for all successful requests.

4. Calculate aggregations of data-centric t-Visibility grouped by replication path.

5. For each replica, create an ordered list of write timestamps in this replica.

---

[1]The module could easily be replaced by changing just one line of code.

6. Create an ordered list of operation end timestamps of all writes.

7. Create the same list for each client using only his writes.

8. For each read request, consider the replicas which were part of the operation result and determine the set of updates which each replica had already committed at the time the read started in the respective replica (based on the results from step 5). Calculate the union of these sets.

9. Use the results from step 6 to look up what the set from step 8 should have looked like. Based on this, flag the request either as stale or fresh.

10. Iterate over the results of step 9 and determine for each write operation W the last read operation L which did not contain the respective write as well as the first read operation F which did contain it. The end timestamp defining client-centric t-Visibility for operation W is within the interval $[t^L_{end}; t^F_{end}]$. Based on this, calculate upper and lower bounds for client-centric t-Visibility.

11. Group the results from step 9 by client, order them by operation end timestamp, and iterate over them. Identify if the union of the results of all operations $< n$ is a subset of the results of operation n. If not flag operation n as being in violation of MRC. Also check whether the results of each operation n with operation end timestamp t^n_{end} contained all writes from step 7 where the respective end timestamp t^i_{end} was smaller than t^n_{end}, i.e., $t^i_{end} < t^n_{end}$. If this is not the case, flag operation n as being in violation of RYWC.

12. Export all analysis results using the *Logging & Utils* module.

Logging & Utils   The *Logging & Utils* module offers support functions for the other modules. Mainly, these are the data structures used for information storage within the *Evaluator* module and several data structures (e.g., custom tree and skip list implementations) to accelerate both the actual Monte Carlo simulation as well as the final analysis of the events.

Apart from these, there is an extensible logging module which saves the simulated events in arbitrary data structures either in memory or on disk. This can be used to analyze event traces generated with our implementation within other tools, e.g., potentially with [81].

Finally, the *Logging & Utils* module comprises several utility classes which can be used to read input data (e.g., values $L_{ij}(s)$) in various input formats and transform it into the format internally used by our simulation tool.

7.2. System Benchmarking

We have also implemented tools to support system benchmarking of client-centric consistency behavior. These tools comprise two simple programs for RYWC and MWC checks as well as a more complex tool for client-centric staleness and MRC measurements which have all been implemented in Java 6. In the following, we describe the implementations of these tools as well as their use within a larger framework for comprehensive system benchmarking of consistency behavior.

7.2.1. RYWC Measurements

RYWC measurements are implemented via the abstract class `AbstractReadYourWrites-ConsistencyChecker` which requires child classes to implement methods for read and write access to the storage system. The abstract class already implements all application logic for the measurement itself so that child classes only have to implement the connector to the storage system.

For measurements, the class is parameterized with the number of tests as well as the minimum number of reads per test. In this case, the number of tests refers to the number of writes whereas the minimum number of reads describes the number of reads without a violation of RYWC before the next test is triggered. Algorithm listing 1 shows the algorithm which we have implemented – it logs the difference in time between write and the respective read plus a 0 for RYWC or a 1 for RYWC violations.

For accurate results, this measurement client should be deployed in a way so that read and write access both have very low latency values.

7.2.2. MWC Measurements

MWC measurements are implemented via the abstract class `AbstractMonotonicWrites-ConsistencyChecker` which requires child classes to implement methods for read and write access to the storage system. The abstract class already implements all application logic for the measurement itself so that child classes only have to implement the connector to the storage system.

For measurements, the class is parameterized with the number of tests (i.e., the number of keys which shall be written) as well as a flag signaling whether the values shall be written or checked. If the flag is not set, the class simply issues two sequential updates to the storage system specified by the child class. In constrast, if the flag is set, the class reads all respective keys and checks whether the returned value is identical to the value of the second write. Finally, results are logged to the console.

input: Number of tests *noTest*, minimum number of reads *minRead*
for $i \leftarrow 1$ **to** *noTest* **do**
    writevalue $\leftarrow i$;
    timestampW $\leftarrow$ getTime();
    writeData(writevalue);
    for $j \leftarrow 1$ **to** *minRead* **do**
        timestampR $\leftarrow$ getTime();
        readvalue $\leftarrow$ readData();
        if readvalue $\geq$ writevalue **then**
            // RYWC is not violated
            log(timestampR $-$ timestampW,*0*);
        else
            // RYWC is violated, restart counter
            log(timestampR $-$ timestampW,*1*);
            $j \leftarrow 1$;
        end
    end
end

Algorithm 1: Measuring RYWC

7.2.3. Staleness and MRC Measurements

As already described in section 6.3, client-centric staleness measurements for both t-Visibility and k-Staleness require a single writer as well as a number of distributed reader machines whereas data-centric staleness measurements require direct access to the storage system. In this section, we describe our implementation of a system benchmarking tool for client-centric staleness measurements which also supports an analysis for MRC violations.

Figure 7.3, which we already introduced in chapter 6, shows the basic test setup for client-centric staleness measurements. Beyond the two presented roles, reader and writer, we also implemented a collector which is deployed on one additional machine. In the following, we start by describing how our system benchmarking tool is started before providing a more detailed overview of each of these roles.

Our system benchmarking tool is parameterized with a URL and a unique ID. The program then proceeds to download a properties file from the specified URL and extracts all necessary information from the generic part of the properties file (e.g., public and private keys for Amazon Web Services[2], the URL of the collector service, the target key etc.).

The specific part of the properties file, in contrast, contains one subsection for every instance, each starting with an ID. Hence, the tool next searches within the properties file for

---

[2]aws.amazon.com

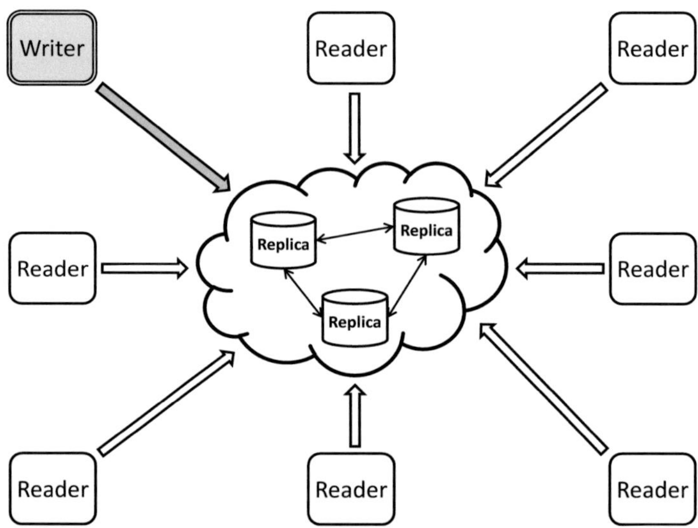

Figure 7.3.: Measurement Setup for Staleness Measurements of Storage Systems with Load Balancer

the ID provided as a parameter and parses the specific configuration information for the respective ID.

There are two mandatory property entries for each ID: `role` and `start`. The `role` value determines which role the instance will assume (e.g., collector), while the `start` property is an integer value. This integer describes the delay value artificially injected before starting the class corresponding to the specified role. This is useful to control the start order of the different machines and, thus, removes the need for a synchronization barrier like Zookeeper[3]. For instance, it is necessary to start the collector first as all other roles will terminate with an error if they cannot reach it. Finally, the respective class is started with all necessary parameters.

Collector   The collector exposes a simple web service interface which accepts a `String` value and two `long` values as parameters. The `String` value corresponds to the ID provided as parameter for each instance, the `long` values to the test number and the observed maximum inconcistency window for that test number. The collector appends these results to a CSV file which can afterwards easily be analyzed using any spreadsheet program.

The results exported by the collector already provide sufficient information to determine client-centric t-Visibility. Beyond these, we have implemented another tool which takes the (typically multi-gigabyte) log files of the reader instances as input and calculates error rates,

---

[3]zookeeper.apache.org

the probability of MRC violations per reader instance, the distribution of read latencies, and the development of fresh versus stale reads (and the corresponding average read latencies) as a function of the time since the last update.

Writer   The writer implements all application logic within an abstract class `Abstract-Writer` which requires child classes to implement the methods `configure(String [ ] params)` and `write(String key, String value)`. The `write()` method has to implement the connector functionality to translate such a method call into an actual request to the respective storage system. For the `configure()` method, the class `AbstractWriter` forwards all parameters beyond the parameters required by the class itself so that arbitrary parameters can be passed to the concrete implementations. Algorithm 2 shows the functionality implemented within class `AbstractWriter`.

---

input: Target key *key*, delay between writes *delay*, additional parameters *params*
`configure`(*params*);
counter ← 0;
while not terminated externally **do**
    timestampStart ← getTime();
    writevalue ← counter + ':' + timestampStart;
    `write`(*key*,writevalue);
    timestampEnd ← getTime();
    `log`(counter,timestampEnd − timestampStart);
    counter ← counter +1;
    `sleep`(*delay*);
end

Algorithm 2: Algorithm in Class `AbstractWriter`

Reader   Comparable to the writer, the reader functionality is again implemented within an abstract class (`AbstractReader`) which requires child classes to implement methods `configure(String [ ] params)` and `read(String key)`. Comparable to the `write()` method, `read()` again has to implement the connector functionality to translate such a method call into an actual request to the respective storage system. For the `configure()` method, surplus parameters are again forwarded so that arbitrary parameters can be passed to the concrete implementations. Algorithm 3 shows the functionality implemented within class `AbstractReader`.

input: Instance ID *id*, target key *key*, delay between reads *delay*, buffer size *buf*,
     additional parameters *params*
`configure(`*params*`);`
while not terminated externally **do**
    timestampStart $\leftarrow$ `getTime();`
    readvalue $\leftarrow$ `read(`*key*`);`
    timestampEnd $\leftarrow$ `getTime();`
    `log(`readvalue,timestampStart,timestampEnd`);`
    `// Put the read result into a map to calculate aggregations for`
    `   the collector`
    testnumber $\leftarrow$ `getTestNumber(`readvalue`);`
    writeTimestamp $\leftarrow$ `getWriteTimestamp(`readvalue`);`
    writeMap.put`(`testnumber,writeTimestamp`);`
    readMap.put`(`testnumber,timestampStart`);`
    counter $\leftarrow$ counter $+1$;
    if counter $\geq buf$ **then**
        `// When the buffer is full (default:  10 entries) calculate`
        `   the maximum staleness for the oldest entry and send it to`
        `   the collector`
        testnumber $\leftarrow$ readMap.getLowestTestnumber`();`
        writeTimestamp $\leftarrow$ writeMap.get`(`testnumber $+1$`);`
        timestampStart $\leftarrow$ readMap.get`(`testnumber`);`
        `sendToCollector(`*id*,testnumber,timestampStart $-$ writeTimestamp`);`
        `// Remove old values to avoid memory issues but keep a few`
        `   older write timestamps to be on the safe side`
        readMap.remove`(`testnumber`);`
        writeMap.remove`(`testnumber -5`);`
        counter $\leftarrow$ counter -1;
    end
    `sleep(`*delay*`);`
end

Algorithm 3: Algorithm in Class `AbstractReader`

7.2.4. Comprehensive System Benchmarking

We have also developed an architecture and a (partial) implementation of a comprehensive system benchmarking framework for consistency behavior. Such a framework should be able to analyze how parallel workloads (i.e., varying resource saturation), geo-replication (i.e., varying latency values for inter-replica communication), node failures (i.e., temporary outages of replicas), and multi-tenancy (i.e., cross-effects between tenants of a cloud storage system) affect the consistency behavior of a storage system.

For this purpose, we propose an architecture offering the following components (see also figure 7.4 for a high-level overview of the proposed architecture):

- Workload Generator: This component is used to create different workloads on the system to allow the quantification of consistency effects during phases of resource saturation. It should also report results for standard performance metrics like latency or throughput to quantify tradeoffs between consistency and performance.

- Tenant Simulator: The *Tenant Simulator* is used to create a specific kind of behavior for individually simulated tenants of a storage system. While the *Workload Generator* just creates load on the system, this component might create a more detailed behavior of a single tenant so that multi-tenant cross-effects on consistency can be studied.

- Consistency Measurement Component (CMC): This is the component which is responsible for measuring the consistency behavior of the underlying system. Its output should use meaningful and fine-grained consistency metrics from a client perspective.

- Failure Injector: The *Failure Injector* is a component which can be used with self-hosted storage systems and can cause a variety of failures.

It could also be reasonable to include a scheduling and deployment component, e.g., [56], to ease measurements of various configurations and systems.

For the actual implementation, we have reused existing, proven tools and patched them together using shell scripts. Our system benchmarking tool presented above is used as the *CMC*.

The Yahoo! Cloud Serving Benchmark (YCSB) [33] is the most well known system benchmarking framework for performance measurements of NoSQL databases. The tool supports different NoSQL databases and various kinds of workloads and has been designed to be extensible in both dimensions. We use it as our *Workload Generator*.

So far, we have not included implementations for a *Tenant Simulator*. We have also not used a *Failure Injector* but Simian Army[4], which was published as open source by Netflix[5], is

---

[4]github.com/Netflix/SimianArmy
[5]netflix.com

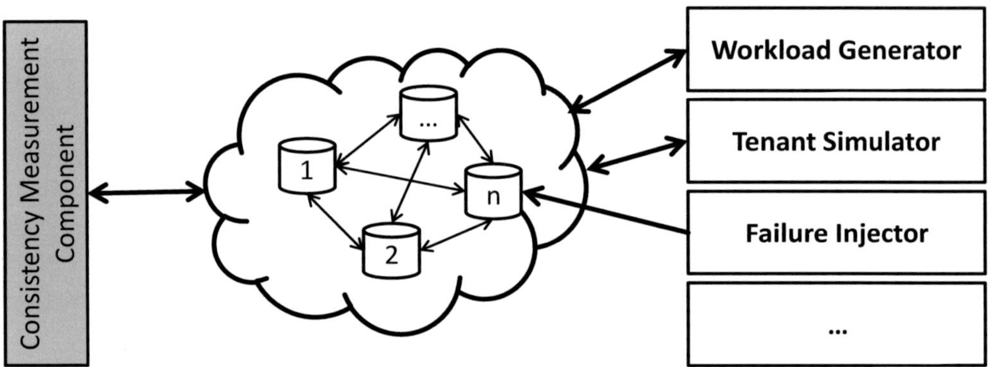

Figure 7.4.: High-level Architecture of our Comprehensive System Benchmarking Framework

a promising candidate for future experiments. Since the loose bundling approach via scripting offers full flexibility and extensibility, this architecture and the implementations which we currently use can be seen as a starting point where each individual component can easily be replaced.

Both our system benchmarking tool and YCSB use an abstract connector architecture so that they can easily be extended for use with different storage systems. We propose to use the same kind of architecture for all other components.

7.3. Running Consistency Benchmarks

This section is intended as a starting point for application developers, researchers or storage developers interested in using one of our Consistency Benchmarking approaches. In the following, we describe the steps necessary if we want to run Consistency Benchmarking. We start with the modeling and simulation approach before describing the setup for our system benchmarking tool.

7.3.1. Modeling and Simulation

After we have identified all interesting systems and their configurations, we have to determine the communication middleware used for communication among the replicas and adapt the ODTT tool from above (cf. section 7.1.1) to use said middleware. We, then, need servers in all datacenters where replicas would be deployed in any of the configurations – this is trivial for cloud-based deployments but can be more difficult for other deployment options. Next, we deploy the ODTT tool on these servers and start it. The tool then collects the data all by itself. After a while, depending on the parameters as well as desired measurement accuracy, we can terminate the tool and download the ODTT results from the servers.

In parallel, we have to obtain estimates for failure rates of servers and network links as well as measurements or estimates for distributions of processing times. Using the information on failures, processing times and the ODTT results, we can then model all systems and configurations in the modeling and simulation tool. Currently, this is done in Java code but implementing a model editor should be straightforward if desired. Afterwards, we can start the simulation run(s) and analyze the resulting CSV output files either programmatically or manually via spreadsheet programs.

7.3.2. System Benchmarking

For system benchmarking, we first have to identify the approximate number and location of replicas – this is trivial for self-deployed NoSQL systems while it may be a bit challenging for cloud storage services. Based on this, we can calculate the necessary number and location of readers. If no adapters for the storage system exist, yet, we have to extend the `Abstract-Writer` and `AbstractReader` classes. Adding new adapters either requires small extensions to the start class or another way to pass necessary input parameters.

After this has been done, we again need access to servers where we deploy our readers, one writer, and one collector – these should be as close as possible to the replicas and also be distributed in a similar way. On these servers, we then start the system benchmark via the enclosed start script and keep it running for a sufficiently long period of time. Afterwards, we can terminate all system benchmarking processes and download the individual output from the servers.

These result files then need to be analyzed – for the output of the collector, we can use any spreadsheet program; for the individual reader results, our framework comes with a command line tool which analyzes the reader files in streaming mode and outputs aggregations which can directly be copied into a spreadsheet.

The procedure for RYWC and MWC measurements is comparable; the only difference is that only one server is needed for those tests and a different main class is used. With regards to the comprehensive system benchmarking, all components beyond the CMC are optional. If, e.g., a Failure Injector is desired, it must be installed on an additional server and started during the system benchmark.

7.4. Discussion and Conclusion

In this chapter, we have provided an overview of our proof of concept implementations. We started by describing our modeling and simulation framework with tools for data gathering, calculating convolutions, and the Monte Carlo simulation approach. Afterwards, we presented our system benchmarking tools for RYWC, MWC, MRC, and client-centric staleness measurements as well as a framework for comprehensive system benchmarking of consistency behavior. We also described, how application or storage developers, researchers or anyone else interested in Consistency Benchmarking results should proceed when using our proof-of-concept implementations.

While each of our tool shows significant progress beyond related work, there are also a few shortcomings due to the their current implementation. As already outlined above, our modeling and simulation tool so far only implements a subset of our approach from chapter 5.

Beyond this, we also use a rather simplistic client implementation in simulations: Before the actual simulation phase starts, this client implementation in class `RandomizedClient` randomly selects start timestamps for all requests based on a uniform distribution. Specifically, this timestamp generation process does *not* consider interdependencies between operations. In actual applications, though, the start timestamps of requests highly depend on both the result as well as the end timestamp of the last request. For instance, if a failure occurs this may either cause the request to abort quickly or to time-out much later – depending on the reason behind the failure as well as the implementation of the application. If the average request latency is lower than the time-out but higher than the latency of the quick abort option, then the latter will actually increase the request rate during failures whereas the first one will decrease the request rate. Our `RandomizedClient` in fact does neither – the request rate stays constant, subject only to small random fluctuations. This as well as other effects heavily affects, as we will see in chapter 8, the accuracy of client-centric consistency simulation.

Regarding our system benchmarking approach, the accuracy of measurement results is obviously limited by the accuracy of NTP or any other clock synchronization protocol used. Furthermore, one might argue that a more complex workload with several concurrent writers and no strict separation between reader and writer roles would be better suited to determine consistency behavior. Still, even strictly consistent storage systems show consistency violations when no isolation mechanisms like locking or transactions are used. At a first glance, this may seem surprising; at a second glance, though, it should be clear that concurrent requests will always lead to consistency violations whenever latency values are larger than zero.

For example, client A reads a data item at time t_0 and writes it back at t_2. In the meantime, client B also writes that data item at time t_1 and later, at time t_3, reads it back. If $t_0 < t_1 < t_2 < t_3$, then the update of client B will be lost even when using a strictly consistent storage system, i.e., during the read at time t_3 and all reads thereafter, RYWC will be violated for client B.

Some inconsistencies are obviously caused by the distributed application workload itself – an effect everyone, who has worked on a document with several other people at the same time, has probably already seen in practice. We, therefore, believe that the measurement workload should rather not try to imitate application workloads. Instead, its goal should be to measure all inconsistencies caused by the storage system, explicitly excluding the ones caused by an application workload. Based on this, we conclude that a more complex workload would not be better for system benchmarking of client-centric consistency behavior.

Furthermore, it is easily possible to have more than one writer as long as there is a synchronization process which asserts that only one write is issued at the same time. This does not affect anything else in the test setup since only the collector communicates with other measurement clients – all other machines are entirely decoupled and work independently. We do not see a different workload in having more than one writer but this could be used to analyze effects of write locality on consistency behavior. Since the collector outputs time series, consistency behavior could then easily be matched with the respective writer location to check for correlation.

8. Evaluation

In this chapter, we present the evaluation results for our contributions from Part II. For this purpose, we start with the evaluation of our modeling and simulation approach in section 8.1 before continuing with our system benchmarking approach in section 8.2. Finally, we close this chapter with a conclusion in section 8.3

This chapter contains material previously published at MW4SOC 2011 [17], TCPTC 2013 [19], and IC2E 2014 [18].

8.1. Modeling and Simulation

For the evaluation of our modeling and simulation approach, we have implemented a custom storage system called Ministorage which we briefly introduce in section 8.1.1. We then deployed Ministorage in various configurations and deployment setups and compared actual consistency behavior to our simulation output for the same configuration and deployment. We specifically decided not to use an existing NoSQL system for several reasons:

1. We can guarantee that Ministorage does not violate any of our assumptions.

2. Ministorage allows to easily inject failures of all kinds and already implements the necessary logging functionality so that a comparison between real and simulated results is possible.

3. Our model allows to mix synchronous and asynchronous update propagation with quorums. To our knowledge, no other storage system exists today where this is possible. We, therefor, need Ministorage to evaluate the entire model.

4. Our simulation tool currently only implements the *Write Set* conflict resolution strategy. We, therefor, also needed a storage system which implements this strategy.

5. Our data collection tool for ODTT values currently uses only our own simple communication middleware. We are working on extending this but meanwhile Ministorage also uses this middleware.

For the evaluation of our data-centric staleness results, we directly compare values obtained via replica logging to our simulation output. We also studied how crash-stop failures

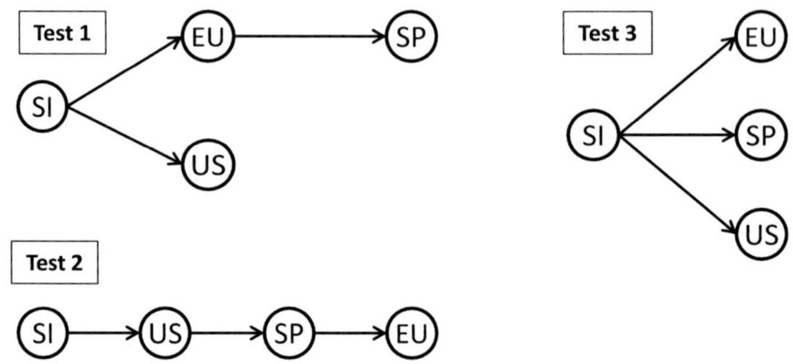

Figure 8.1.: MiniStorage's Replication Graphs during Tests 1, 2 and 3

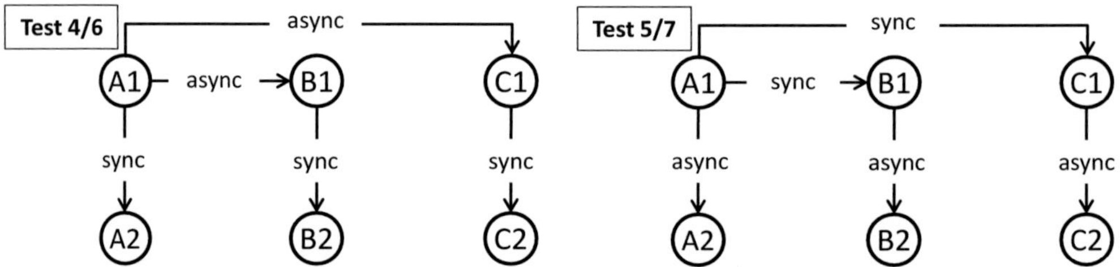

Figure 8.2.: MiniStorage's Replication Graphs during Tests 4, 5, 6 and 7 for replica A1

of replicas affect data-centric staleness. As, for several reasons, our simulation implementation can only provide qualitative but not quantitative predictions for all other metrics, we have analyzed how the replication factor affects MRC and RYWC and how geo-replication affects both data-centric and client-centric staleness.

8.1.1. MiniStorage

MiniStorage has been implemented as a system benchmarking testbed for consistency behavior. In its original version it was a simple quorum system and was used to measure the accuracy of our system benchmarking approach [17]. Since then it has evolved to a key-value store that typically keeps data in memory and offers both *Write Set* and *Last Write Wins* conflict resolution strategies. Arbitrary numbers of replication graphs can be specified, though, read graphs may currently contain only one replica. Beyond a CRUD interface it also supports record append operations inspired by the Google File System [44] which we need for the *Write Set* conflict resolution strategy. Failed requests on asynchronous connections are retried until they complete, on synchronous connections the operation fails. The system allows to inject all kinds of failures and implements the staged event-driven architecture [99]. Users can specify whether the system shall expose dirty reads or not.

Table 8.1.: Basic Test Setup Parameters in Comparison

Test No.	Distribution	Setup	# Replication Graphs	Update Operation	MTBF	MTTR
1	WAN	MS	1	put	-	-
2	WAN	MS	1	put	-	-
3	WAN	MS	1	put	-	-
4	LAN	P2P	6	record append	-	-
5	LAN	P2P	6	record append	-	-
6	LAN	P2P	6	record append	3min	10s
7	LAN	P2P	6	record append	30s	10s
8	LAN	P2P	1-6	record append	-	-

8.1.2. Test Setup

We evaluated our approach using both single site and geo-distributed deployments running on top of EC2 small instances[1]. We used the data gathering tool described in section 7.1.1 to measure ODTT values for both test setups before actually running the tests.

Tests 1, 2 and 3 (WAN) For the geo-distributed deployment we started one instance each in the regions us-east (US), eu-west (EU), sao-paulo (SP) and singapore (SI). We then added only one replication graph, i.e., used a master-slave setup, with the master running in the singapore region. Figure 8.1 shows the respective replication graph we used for tests 1, 2 and 3. All updates were propagated asynchronously. Our client was running in Karlsruhe, Germany and issued 1000 write requests per test run. Each test was repeated several times with the same outcome.

Tests 4, 5, 6 and 7 (LAN) For the single site deployment we started two instances each in all three availability zones in the region eu-west. We use the names A1 and A2 to refer to the instances running in availability zone A etc. We configured MiniStorage in a P2P setting, i.e., added one replication graph per instance. For tests 4 and 6, the start replica forwarded its updates synchronously to the other replica in the same zone and asynchronously forwarded the request to one replica in each of the other two availability zones. This instance, in turn, forwarded the request synchronously to the other replica in the same zone. So, essentially, update propagation within the availability zone was synchronous while traffic to other availability zones was asynchronous. For tests 5 and 7, this was configured exactly the other way around. Figure 8.2 shows the replication graphs for replica A1 as an example. All

---

[1] aws.amazon.com/ec2

other replication graphs were configured likewise. For the LAN tests, MiniStorage was set to avoid dirty reads.

During tests 5 and 7, we repeatedly failed node B1, resulting in MTBF of about 3 minutes for test 5 and of about 30 seconds for test 7. The MTTR in both cases was 10 seconds.

To create load on the system, we implemented a sample application mimicking an Internet forum. The application continuously triggers either a read (randomly) or uses the record append operation to add a post. We deployed this application on one instance each in all three availability zones, issuing between 500 and 5000 record appends per client[2].

Test 8 (LAN)   We ran an additional set of tests to evaluate our client-centric ordering simulations. For this purpose, we deployed Ministorage on six EC2 small instances in the region eu-west (two instances per availability zone) and configured our instances to forward updates to all other nodes asynchronously (this corresponds to a (N,R,W) configuration of (N,1,1)). As load generator, we used the same sample application as in tests 4 to 7 running on three small instances. Requests were routed to a randomly chosen replica and were executed sequentially per client (i.e., a new operation would only start after the end of the last operation). For the actual test, we first used only one Ministorage instance in zone A. Next, we added a replica in zone B, then zone C and so on. The purpose of this test was to analyze the influence of the replication factor on MRC and RYWC via both system benchmarking and simulation.

Table 8.1 gives an overview of the different setups for tests 1 to 8.

8.1.3. Results

Figures 8.3 to 8.9 give an overview of our evaluation results for tests 1 to 7, all plotted curves are moving averages over 50ms intervals. Figures 8.11 and 8.12 show the results of test 8.

As already mentioned in section 5.3.3, we encountered some difficulties in accurately determining the distribution of processing times as those values seem to depend on the structure of replication graphs used. Therefore, we used only the average value in simulations instead of a distribution function (i.e., we ignored the variance) as we preferred to use *no* variance compared to a *wrong* variance value. This allows us to make an educated guess in advance regarding the deviation of system benchmarking and simulation results which is useful for showing that the approach actually works. When using our simulation approach to determine actual consistency behavior for application engineering, it, of course, makes sense to estimate a variance value.

---

[2]The actual number was chosen randomly. In the beginning, each of our tests issued 1000 requests per client; later, each client issued 10,000 requests.

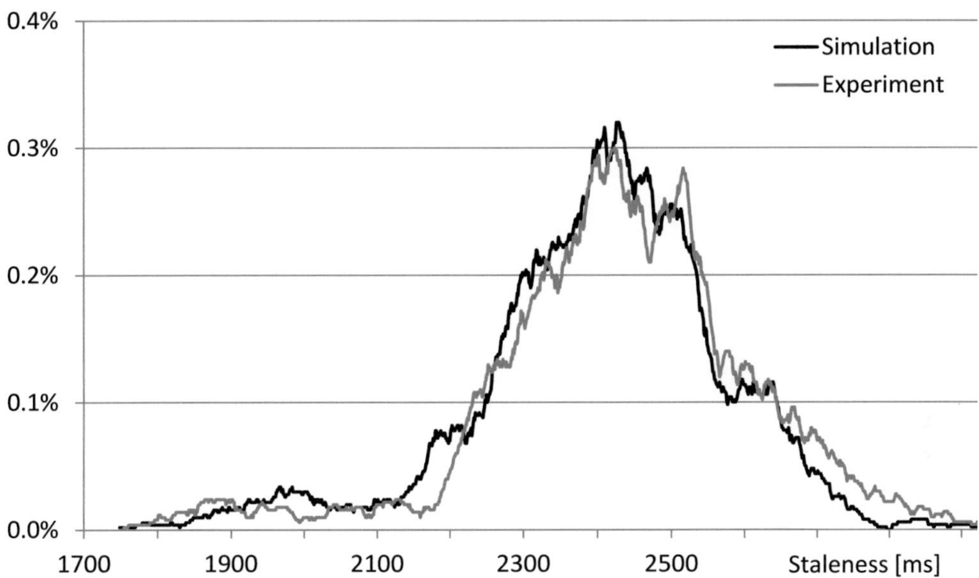

Figure 8.3.: Density Functions of Measured and Simulated Data-centric Staleness in Test 1

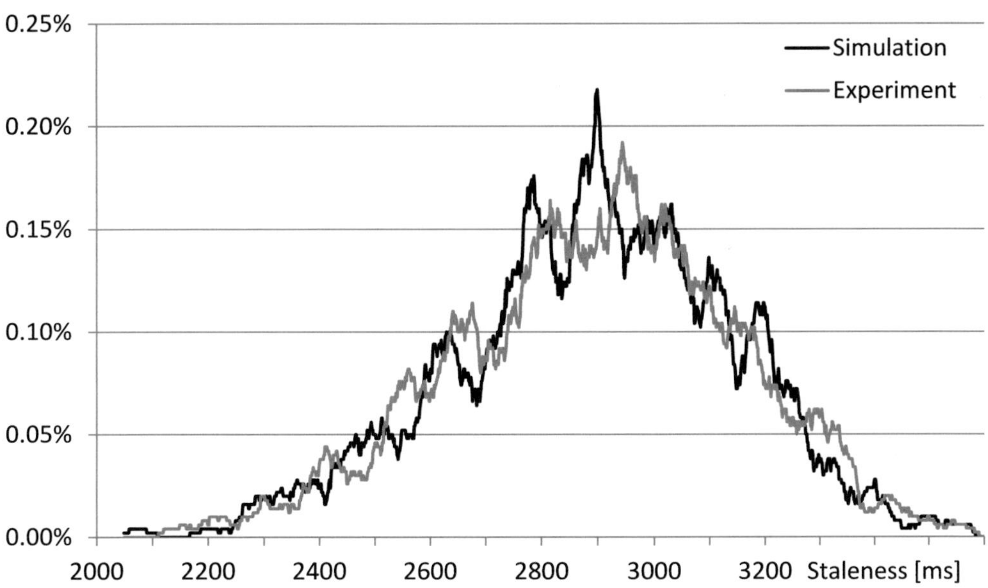

Figure 8.4.: Density Functions of Measured and Simulated Data-centric Staleness in Test 2

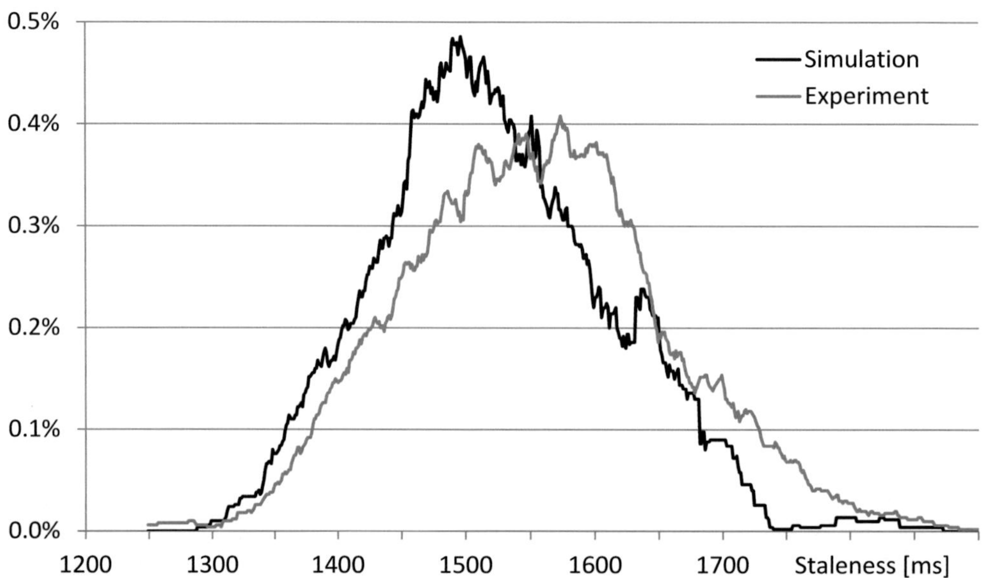

Figure 8.5.: Density Functions of Measured and Simulated Data-centric Staleness in Test 3

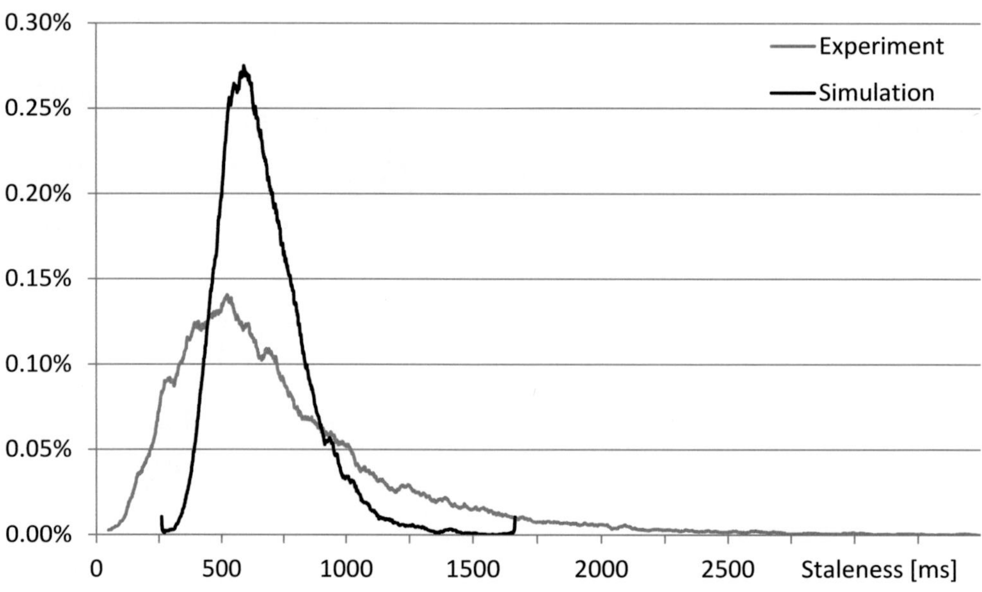

Figure 8.6.: Density Functions of Measured and Simulated Data-centric Staleness in Test 4

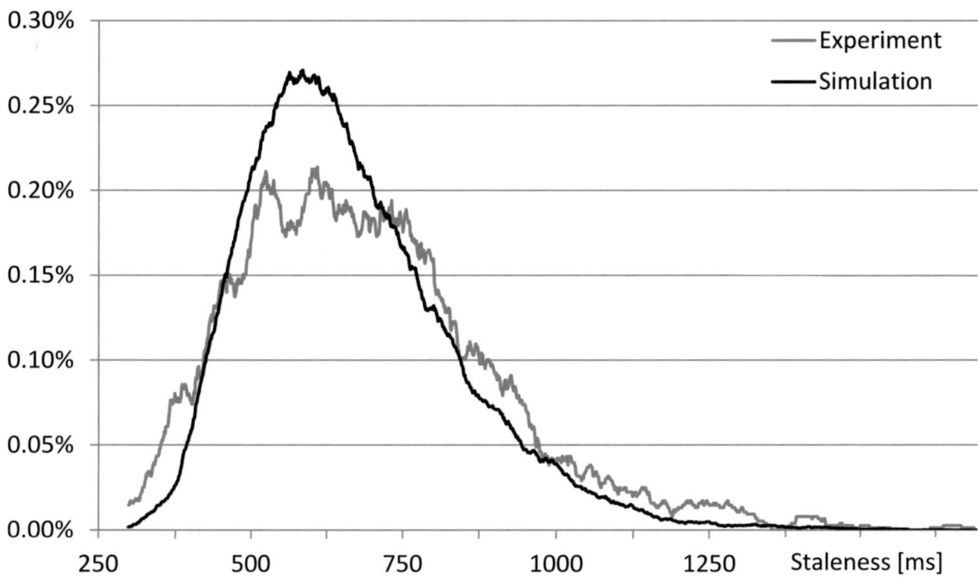

Figure 8.7.: Density Functions of Measured and Simulated Data-centric Staleness in Test 5

This can also be seen in the results: While figures 8.3, 8.4 and 8.5 show almost identical curves for both simulation and experiment, figures 8.6 and 8.8 show a simulated distribution with less variance compared to the experiment. This is due to the fact, that during tests 1, 2 and 3 the relative error caused by inaccurate processing times is low due to wide area replication with high ODTT values. For tests 5 and 7 in contrast (different setup than tests 4 and 6) the processing times distribution actually *has* a low variance value. This is caused by the the fact that asynchronous update propagation across data centers (tests 4 and 6) is more likely to encounter an error, thus, causing a retry which increases the processing time overhead. For synchronous replication the request just fails and is no longer considered in the curve which asserts a lower variance level for tests 5 and 7. It will be an interesting issue to study in future work, how processing times are influenced by replication graphs. Still, median and average values are fairly close (see figure 8.10).

Another influence on the variance of those tests are failures: While not considered in the model (i.e., we simulated a situation without failures) we cannot rule out that failures occurred during our experiment causing a retry or a delayed request. A lesson learned from this is that it is important to include accurate failure modeling for all components.

Regarding tests with artificially induced failures, both simulation and experiment show the expected results: A failure duration of ten seconds causes a "long tail" with a length of ten seconds beyond the median value. The "thickness" of the tail depends on the number of requests processed during the failure situation. Here, our average values deviate for simulation and experiment as (which we discovered after the test runs) the test application and the simulation tool handle requests differently: While the simulation tool continuously creates requests independent of failures, a real application client may block briefly during failure situations and, thus, create less requests while failures persist. Or a real application client may fail quickly (faster than the average operation latency) and actually create more requests during failure situations.

This can be seen in figure 8.10: the setup of test 6 causes most requests to reach the failed node asynchronously so that the application client can continue to issue requests, whereas in the setup of test 7 the application contacts B1 mainly synchronously so that the client blocks briefly before the operation fails. This causes the experiment client to issue more requests than the simulation client in test 6 and less requests in test 7 which causes the discrepancy of the average values.

This is a flaw in the implementation of the client model in our simulation tool (and not a flaw in the model itself), we are not yet sure how best to consider this fact in simulations.

For the sake of completeness, we also repeated tests 1, 2 and 3 using not our Monte Carlo simulation approach but instead calculating convolutions. The results showed no recognizable deviation from the Monte Carlo results presented above.

Just as with failures, client-centric behavior heavily depend on the client workload. As a detailed workload model is not part of our consistency model (and to our knowledge no sufficiently precise model exists yet) so that our implementation also includes a rather simplistic client simulation, we can only provide qualitative results. Still, we believe that the simulation approach itself produces accurate quantitative results for the simulated workload, i.e., if a client model accurately reflects the behavior of a real client, then the simulation output will also provide quantitatively correct results. Still, at the moment we cannot prove this. As we have also seen in many system benchmarks, the client-observable consistency behavior is highly volatile with respect to changes in the client workload pattern so that small deviations in the implementation details of real and simulated clients cause severe deviations for the simulation and measurement outputs. To further highlight this, figures 8.11 and 8.12 show two different simulated workloads: Simulation 1 had three clients which each issued 15 read and 15 write requests per second (i.e., a total of 90 operations per second); simulation 2 also had three clients but each of those clients issued 20 read and 20 write requests per second (i.e., a total of 120 operations per second). As expected, both simulation and system benchmark show that increasing the replication factor also increases the probability of MRC and RYWC violations.

We also studied how geo-replication (manifested in higher ODTT values) affects client-centric and data-centric t-Visibility levels. From past experiments, we know (see also the

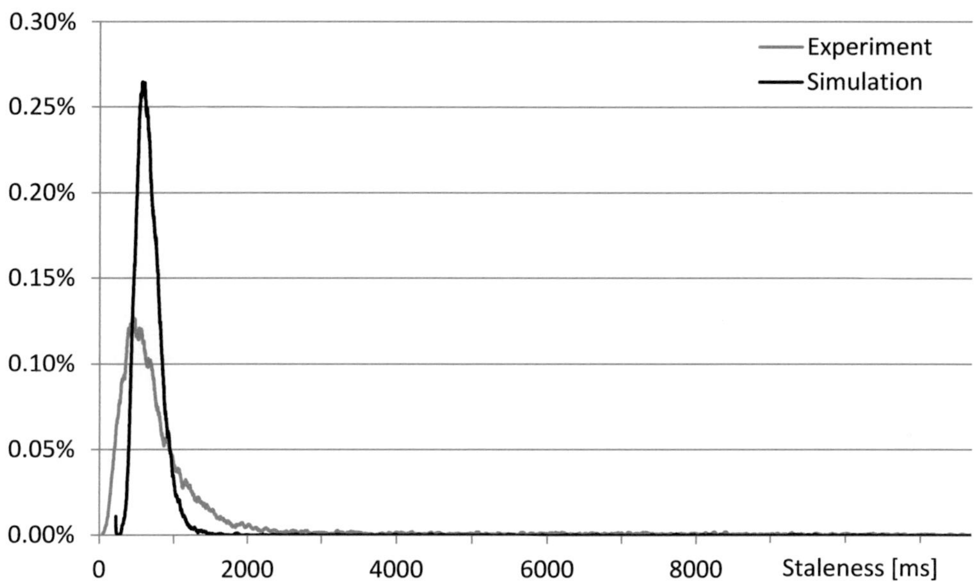

Figure 8.8.: Density Functions of Measured and Simulated Data-centric Staleness in Test 6

experiments in section 8.2) that this leads to higher t-Visibility values – both from a client and a provider perspective. In large numbers of simulation runs in various configurations, we have seen that to be true for each simulation output without any doubt. When calculating convolutions, this could even be shown mathematically. We, therefore, do not report detailed results of these simulation runs here.

8.2. System Benchmarking

This section is divided into three parts: We start with a comparison of data-centric staleness behavior obtained via replica logging in Ministorage and client-centric staleness values measured using our system benchmarking approach. In that test, we varied the number of readers to actually show our numeric simulation results from figure 6.1 (chapter 6) in practice. As a second evaluation part, we have conducted a long-term experimental study of Amazon S3[3]. Finally, the third part is an analysis of how parallel workloads and geo-replication affect consistency behavior in MongoDB[4] and Apache Cassandra[5].

---

[3] aws.amazon.com/s3
[4] mongodb.org
[5] cassandra.apache.org

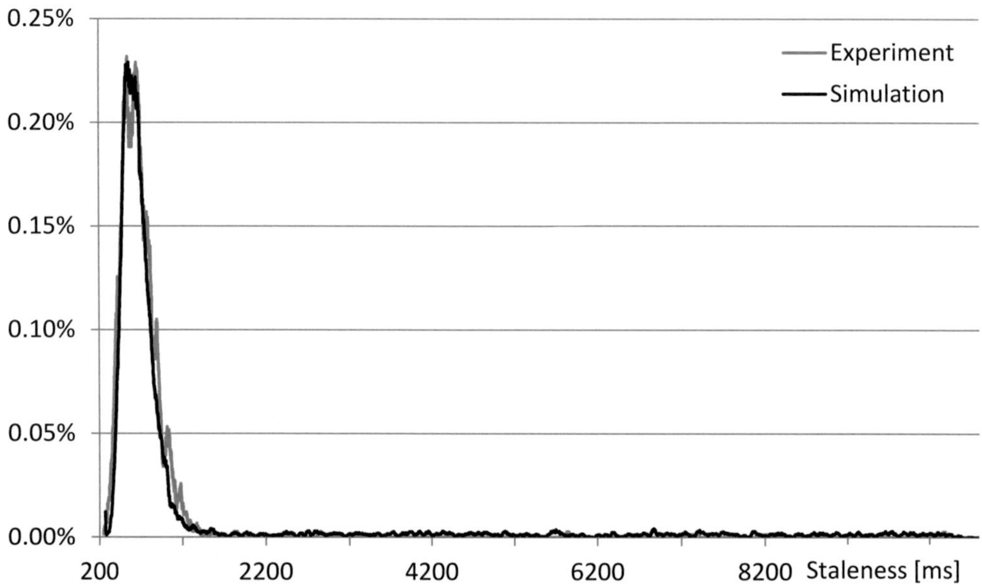

Figure 8.9.: Density Functions of Measured and Simulated Data-centric Staleness in Test 7

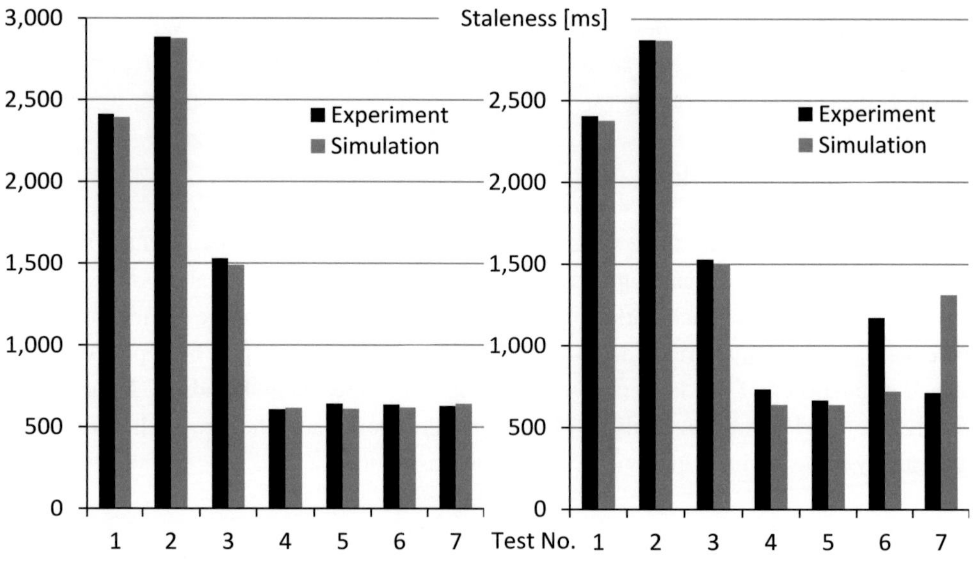

Figure 8.10.: Median (Left) and Average (Right) Results of System Benchmark and Simulation

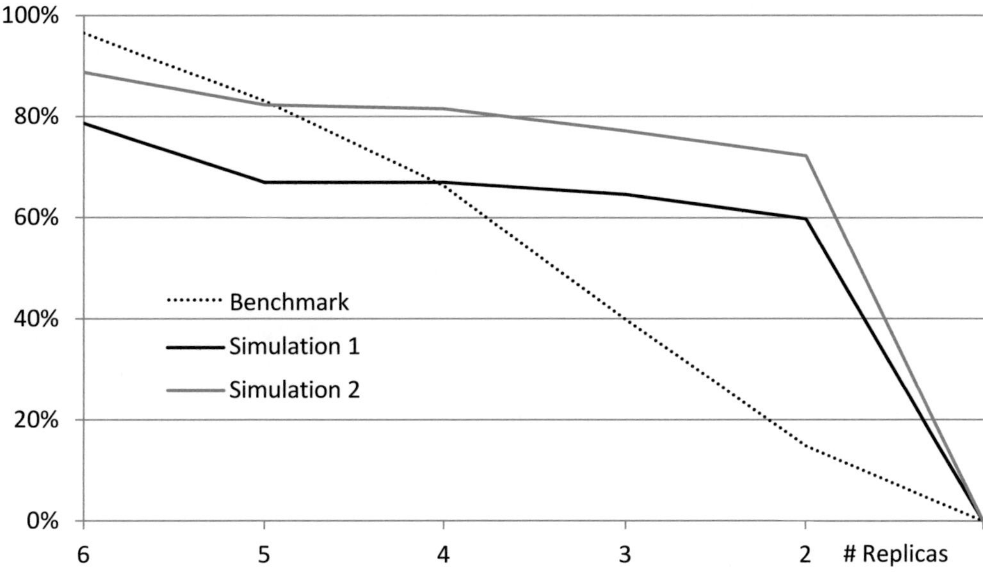

Figure 8.11.: Average Percentage of MRC Violations in Test 8

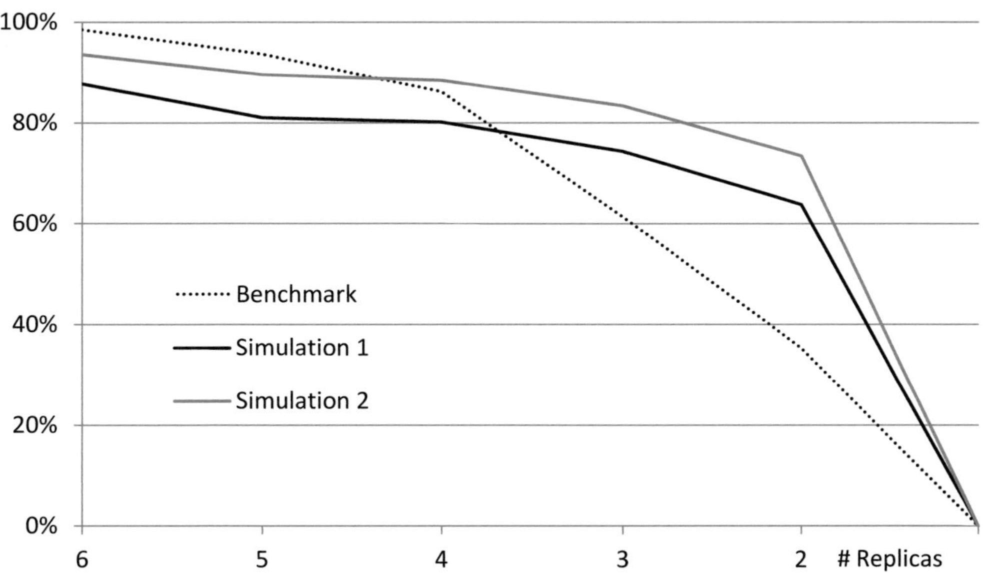

Figure 8.12.: Average Percentage of RYWC Violations in Test 8

8.2.1. Data-centric and Client-centric Staleness

As already discussed in chapter 6, the accuracy of our system benchmarking approach highly depends on the number of readers used. This becomes clear when looking at the probability of reaching all replicas: For example, in a scenario with three replicas where a load balancer routes requests to a randomly chosen replica (uniformly distributed) we assume that all readers read only once at the same time. In that case, there is a probability of less than 4% of reaching all replicas when using the minimum number of three readers. When using more readers, this value increases to 83% (for seven readers) or 93% (for nine readers). This in turn implies that data-centric staleness is an upper bound for client-observable inconsistency windows since there is always a chance of missing one replica, i.e., the probability of reading all replica will always be less than 100%. It is possible to calculate these probability values mathematically, still the set of assumptions above leaves a level of uncertainty whether the number of readers used suffices for a particular usecase. In this section, we study this experimentally.

To address this question, we again used Ministorage (section 8.1.1), this time in a quorum configuration with a replication level of three. Each read request was served by just one replica. Write requests also terminated after committing the update locally. After this, we injected an artificial one second delay[6] before forwarding the write request to the other two replicas. This corresponds to an (N,R,W) configuration of (3,1,1) [97]. We used replica logging to determine the data-centric staleness behavior.

For our evaluation, we deployed Ministorage on three Amazon EC2 small instances within the region us-east, each running in different availability zones. Next, we deployed our system benchmarking tool on EC2. The writer, the collector and the first readers were deployed in the same availability zone as the first replica. For our test, we used an update interval of five seconds and a read interval of ten milliseconds. Afterwards, we added another reader every 10 minutes. While the first reader was in availability zone A, the second was in B, the third in C, the fourth in A again, and so on. We did this until we had twelve readers running. At that point we stopped adding readers but kept the system running for another two hours.

The test results show a fairly stable data-centric t-Visibility of slightly above one second. At the same time, our consistency measurements slowly approach that curve asymptotically. This proves the validity of our considerations regarding both the number of readers necessary to reach all replicas with a certain probability as well as regarding the upper bounds for client-centric staleness.

Figure 8.13 shows our measurement results; the grey bar stands for data-centric staleness while the black bar shows our measured results gained by adding more and more readers.

---

[6]Originally, observed system latencies and inconsistency windows were close to the accuracy range of NTP which we use for clock synchronization so that no meaningful results could be achieved.

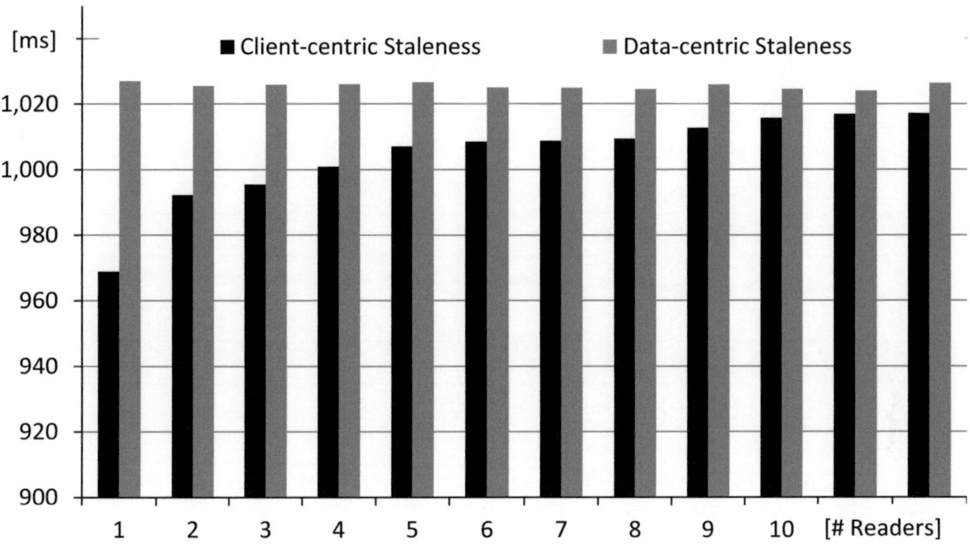

Figure 8.13.: Data-centric versus Client-observable Inconsistency Windows with Varying Number of Readers

To remove small random fluctuations the figure only shows the mean values for each period between changing the number of readers. The actual values nevertheless contained not even one outlier which exceeded the data-centric staleness. From this experiment, we can also see that beyond a certain number of readers it becomes highly inefficient to achieve higher accuracy.

8.2.2. Long-term Study with Amazon S3

In this section, we present the results of our long-term experimental study using Amazon S3 as an example. We start by describing the results our staleness measurements over time before continuing to other measurement results.

Staleness and MRC Results

For each of our experiments, we deployed twelve readers on EC2 small instances in the AWS region eu-west, four each in every availability zone; we also deployed a writer instance in zone A. In our experiments, we varied both the test duration (24 hours or 7 days) and the interval between updates (10 or 20 seconds), see table 8.2.

Table 8.2.: Experiment Setups

Experiment	Start Date	Duration	Write Interval	Commment
1	Aug 29, 2011	7d	10s	-
2	Nov 10, 2011	24h	20s	one reader crashed
3	Nov 16, 2011	24h	20s	-
4	Nov 17, 2011	24h	10s	-
5	Oct 2, 2012	24h	10s	-
6	Oct 3, 2012	7d	10s	-
7	Sept 4, 2013	24h	10s	-
8	Sept 6, 2013	7d	10s	-

In experiment 1[7], we observed the two periodicities already reported in our original paper [17]: Alternating LOW and SAW phases which we later determined to be correlated to working hours since the experiment started at Monday morning, 10.30h local time. Figure 8.14 shows how the maximum observable t-Visibility values change over time. During the SAW phases ("black areas" in figure 8.14) staleness values changed in a sawtooth pattern with a wavelength of slightly below two minutes. Figure 8.15 shows a randomly selected excerpt from a SAW phase. The rest of the time, i.e., during the LOW phases, values were as expected distributed randomly. We believe, also based on experiments where multiple files were targeted with system benchmarks at the same time, that the S3 implementation at that time initiated update propagation either periodically or upon a second write to the same bucket.

On October 20, 2011, we contacted Amazon regarding this behavior. While they would not comment on the root source of this effect, they quickly made changes to their implementation which we were able to observe in experiments 2, 3 and 4: While the daily patterns were still clearly visible (see figure 8.16, the chart has been clipped at about 15 seconds) and the LOW phase had not changed, the SAW phase showed an "obscurified" but still recognizable sawtooth pattern, see figure 8.17 for a randomly selected excerpt from the SAW phase[8]. Interestingly, the median of the staleness values increased so that the update actually decreased the consistency behavior in that dimension.

Almost one year later, we again benchmarked S3 – a 24 hour experiment and another 7 day experiment to verify our findings. Amazon must have made additional changes to their system as the daily/weekly patterns of SAW and LOW phases did not exist any longer.

---

[7]We actually repeated this experiment several times with the same behavior.
[8]Experiments 2,3 and 4 showed almost identical results.

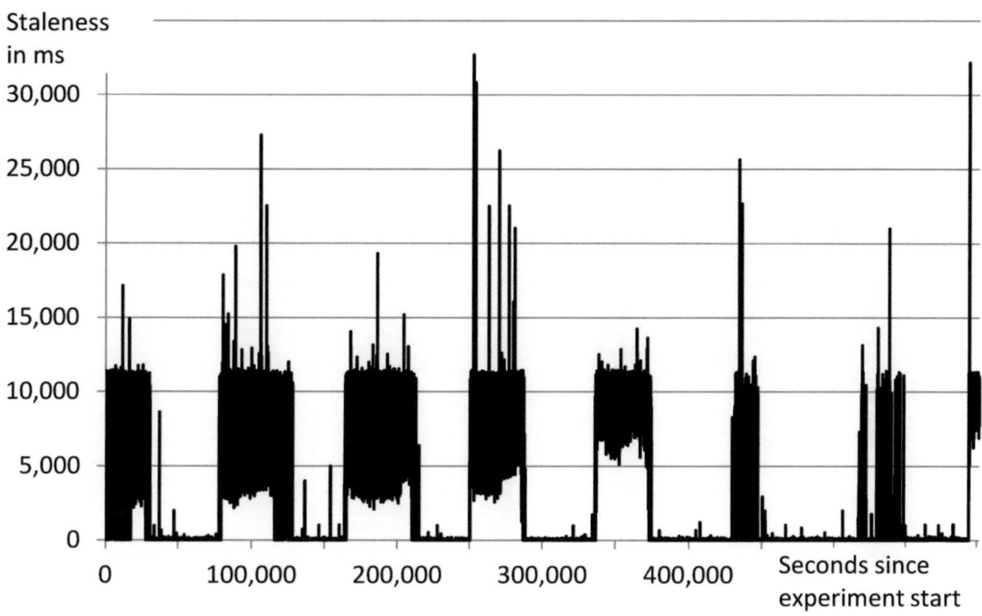

Figure 8.14.: SAW and LOW Phases in Experiment 1

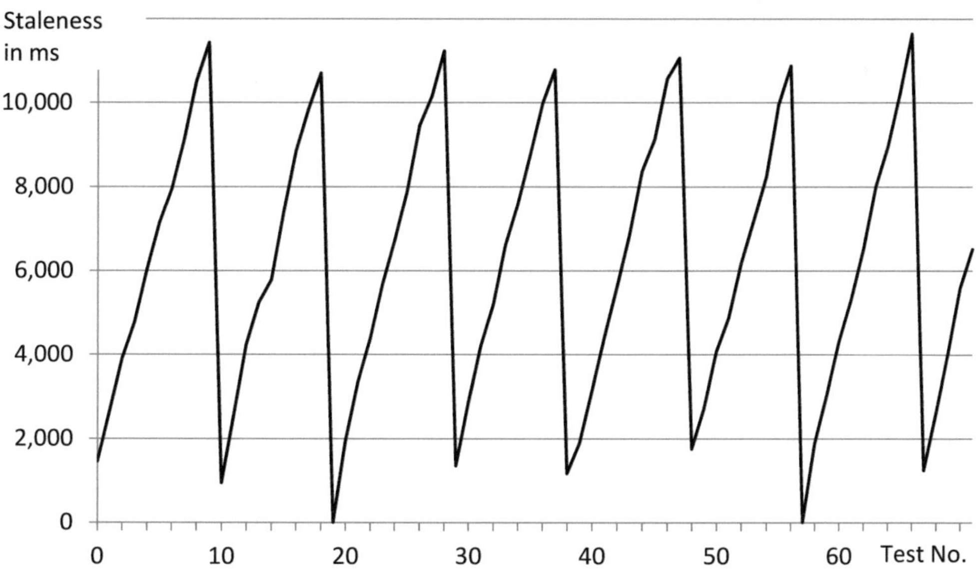

Figure 8.15.: Excerpt from a SAW Phase in Experiment 1

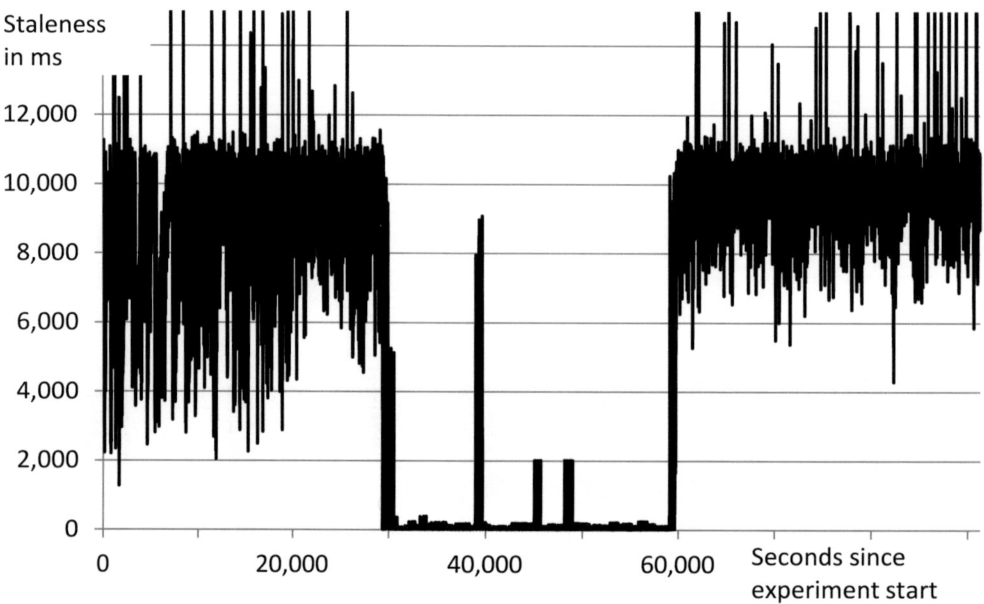

Figure 8.16.: SAW and LOW Phases in Experiment 4

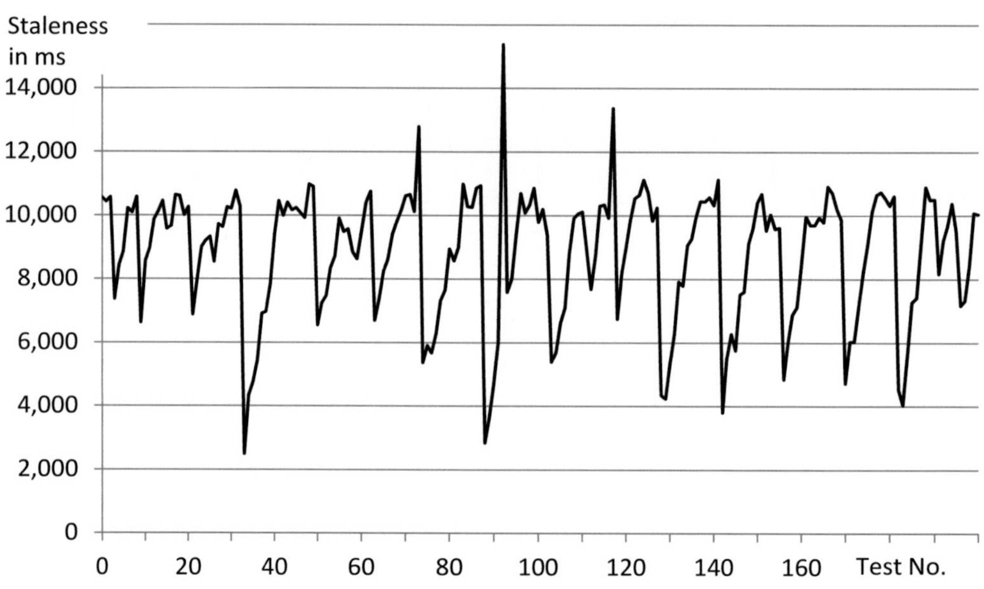

Figure 8.17.: Excerpt from a SAW Phase in Experiment 4

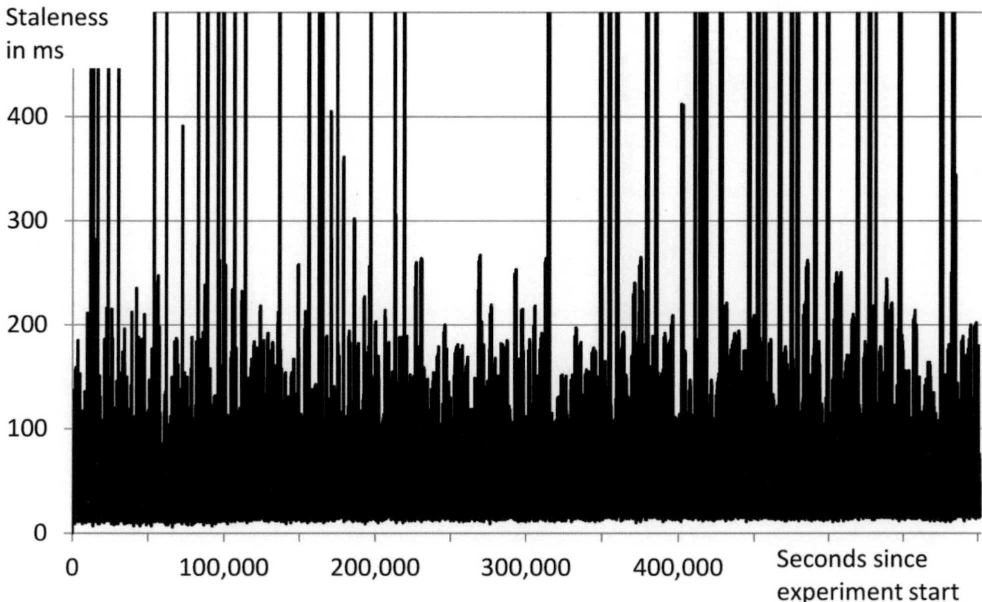

Figure 8.18.: Staleness Results of Experiment 6

Furthermore, even maximum peak values did not exceed 10 seconds any more; in fact, most peaks were below one second. Figure 8.18 shows the results of experiment 6[9]; the chart has been clipped at 500ms – still, we could count less than 50 peaks of more than one second out of 60,000 measurements. This was actually the behavior we would have expected for our original experiments in 2011.

Another year later, in September 2013, we repeated experiments 5 and 6. During these experiments we observed that the number of peaks had increased dramatically. Furthermore, even though these peaks were typically between 6 and 10 seconds, there were also quite a few peaks still exceeding 10 seconds of staleness. Average values increased by about 100ms, median values doubled and standard deviation values increased between 300% and 600% compared to experiments 5 and 6. While results are still far better than in 2011, they are now, in 2013, effectively worse than in 2012. Especially, the increase in variance has caused the consistency behavior to become much more unpredictable. Figure 8.19 shows the results of staleness measurements in experiment 7[10].

Figure 8.20 and table 8.3 show how the aggregated results have evolved over time.

---

[9]Experiment 5 showed almost identical behavior.
[10]When comparing figures 8.18 and 8.19, note that figure 8.19 uses a logarithmic scale.

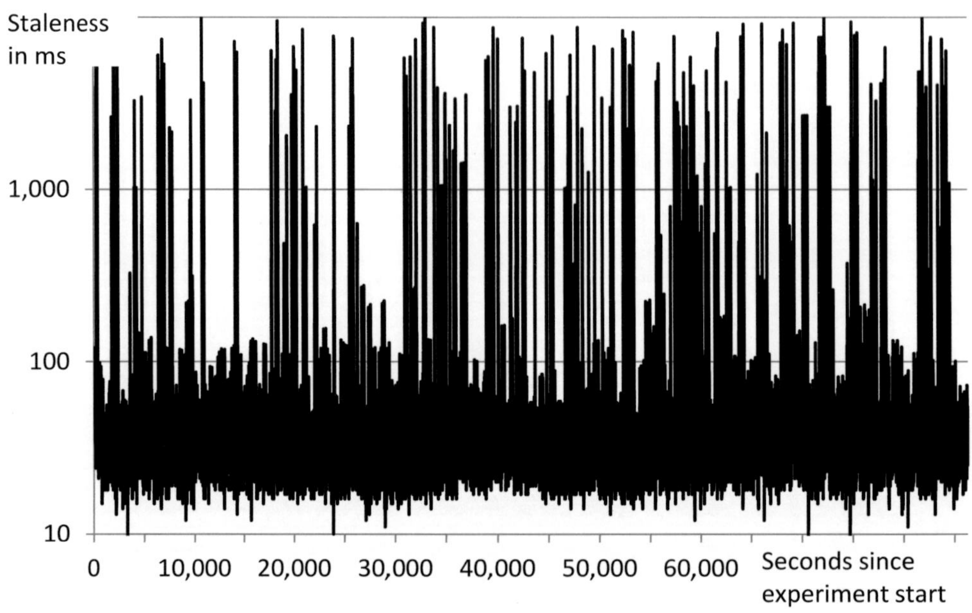

Figure 8.19.: Staleness Results of Experiment 7

While analyzing the results of experiment 8, we also discovered a curious "bump" in the chart showing the probability of reading non-stale data as a function of time since the last update (see figure 8.21). When we went back to also recheck the results of the other seven experiments, we realized that they all had the same "bump" in the very same time interval. Further analysis revealed that there is also a temporary increase in average read latency values right before the "bump" (see figure 8.22 which shows the read throughput as well as the average read latency over time). As this behavior keeps reoccurring in all eight experiments of which experiment 8 alone is based on more than half a billion reads, we believe that this is not random behavior.

Obviously, the increased read latency affects only fresh reads while stale reads continue unaffectedly. The only explanation that we can come up with, is that about 30ms after an update started (we have single digit update latencies), the only existing fresh replica blocks briefly to update another replica, while a third (still stale) replica continues to serve requests.

Recently, we also extended our system benchmarking approach to measure the inconsistency window of delete operations, i.e., how long a value is still readable after having been deleted. In the results of several experiments, we noted that there is no effect on staleness of deletes caused by the workload executed before the delete operation. This indicates that Amazon uses a constant number of replicas independent of the actual workload on a specific

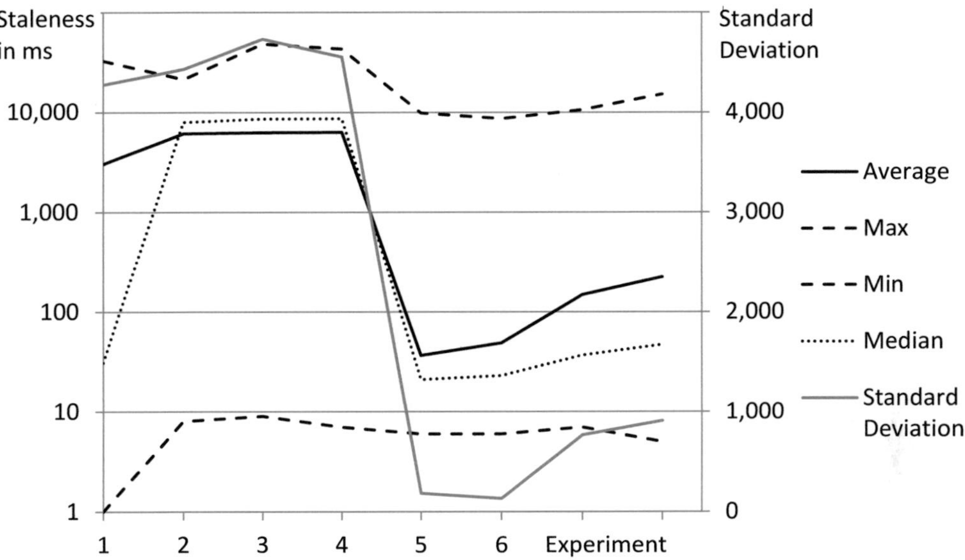

Figure 8.20.: Overview of Results in Experiments 1-8

Table 8.3.: Results of Experiments 1-8

Experiment	Min. [ms]	Avg. [ms]	Median [ms]	Max. [ms]	Std. Dev. [ms]
1	1	3,029.48	31	32,716	4,276.60
2	8	6,072.17	7,969	21,439	4,431.88
3	9	6,220.37	8,603	48,281	4,731.92
4	7	6,277.14	8,648.5	42,922	4,553.42
5	6	36.65	21	9,854	183.62
6	6	48.81	23	8,663	132.10
7	7	147.77	37	10,594	767.56
8	5	223.14	47	15,165	908.35

key. It is, therefore, also unlikely that Amazon uses caching layers in S3. The results of our delete experiments were comparable to the results of experiments 7 and 8 so that it seems likely that delete and update operations are implemented in a similar way.

As already mentioned, our approach for staleness measurements also logs the results of MRC violations and read error rates. Table 8.4 gives an overview of the results. Note, that the MRC results of experiments 2 and 3 have to be normalized as most updates complete below 10 seconds so that during the second half of the update interval MRC guarantees can

Table 8.4.: MRC and Error Results of Experiments 1-8

Experiment	% Prob. of MRC Violations	Prob. of Read Errors
1	12.0461%	$2.8 * 10^{-9}$
2	4.8603%	$7.2 * 10^{-7}$
3	5.0634%	$3 - 6 * 10^{-5}$
4	10.6982%	$6.8 * 10^{-5}$
5	0.0013%	$3.1 * 10^{-7}$
6	0.0005%	10^{-7}
7	0.0359%	$5 * 10^{-8}$
8	0.0364%	$7.3 * 10^{-8}$

only be violated if there is a peak value with a staleness value beyond 10 seconds. A rough approximation of the normalized results is to multiply the measured values with a factor of two, thus, simply excluding all staleness values beyond 10 seconds.

Based on these results, we can see that the original Amazon update slightly improved MRC behavior before really driving the rate of MRC violations down in 2012 where we also had the best staleness results. In our 2013 experiments, we then again saw an increase in MRC violations – while the values continue to be low, they still increased by a factor of approximately 30 between 2012 and 2013.

Further Results

We also measureed MWC and RYWC violations. For this purpose, we deployed a single EC2 small instance in the Amazon region eu-west. For the MWC measurements, this instance issued an update and directly afterwards issued another update to the same key. We did this for 1000 keys. Afterwards, we periodically checked over the course of 24 hours whether the value that could be read was identical to the value of the second update. Neither of these checks returned the value of the first update so that the result of our experiment was, hence, that MWC seems guaranteed by S3. We ran this system benchmark on March 19, 2012 and September 4, 2013.

On the same dates we also ran our RYWC system benchmark where we first issued a write and then read this value back 100 times. This was repeated for 1000 writes and never read any value older than the one our client had just written. We, therefore, conclude that S3 also seems to guarantees RYWC.

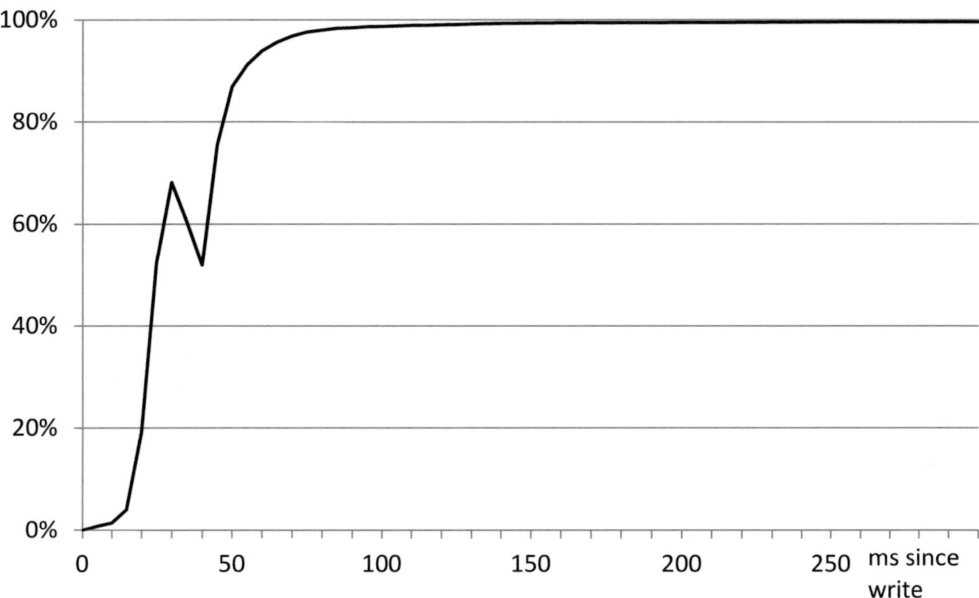

Figure 8.21.: Prob. of Reading Fresh Data as a Function of the Time since the Last Update (Exp. 8)

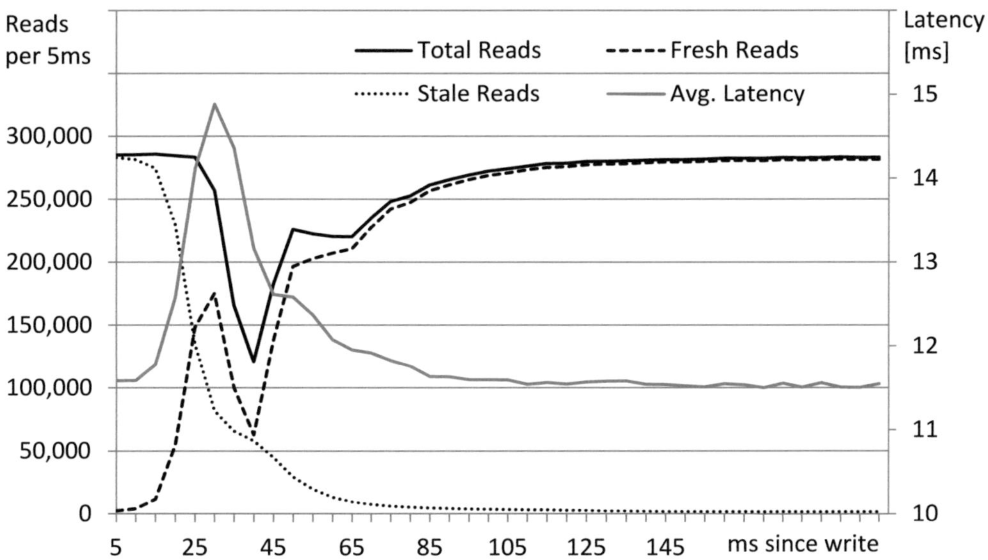

Figure 8.22.: Influence of the Time since the Last Update on Latency and Read Rates (Experiment 8)

Setup		Workload			
System	Replica Type	idle	CMC only	read-heavy	update-heavy
Cassandra	Update Coordinator	<5%	ca. 20%	70-80%	70-80%
	Other Replica	<5%	15-20%	ca. 25%	25-40%
MongoDB	Master	<5%	20%	ca. 25%	35-40%
	Slave	<5%	5-10%	ca. 25%	35-40%

Table 8.5.: CPU Utilization During System Benchmarks for Consistency Behavior

8.2.3. Geo-replication and Parallel Workloads

To show the applicability of our framework for comprehensive system benchmarking of consistency behavior which we presented in section 7.2.4, we studied how geo-distribution of replicas combined with two different workloads affects the consistency behavior of Cassandra and MongoDB. We chose these NoSQL systems as Cassandra is a popular example of P2P systems whereas MongoDB is typically (and was during our tests) configured in a master-slave setup.

Experiment Setup

In our experiments, we ran the following three system benchmarks on Amazon EC2[11], each with Cassandra and MongoDB:

- Single-AZ: All replicas were deployed in the region *eu-west* within the same availability zone[12].

- Multi-AZ: One replica was deployed in each of the three availability zones of the region *eu-west*.

- Multi-Region: One replica was deployed in three different regions: *eu-west*, *us-west* (northern California) and *asia-pacific* (Singapore).

All replicas were deployed on m1.medium instances, whereas our writer and readers were running on m1.small instances distributed according to the respective test. YCSB was deployed on an m1.xlarge instance. Both YCSB and the writer machine of the Consistency Measurement Component (CMC) as well as the MongoDB master were deployed in the eu-west-1a availability zone. We used a simple load balancer strategy for all tests, where

---

[11] aws.amazon.com/ec2

[12] On AWS, availability zones describe completely independent data centers located next to each other within the same geographical region. AWS regions each have at least two availability zones and are geographically distributed.

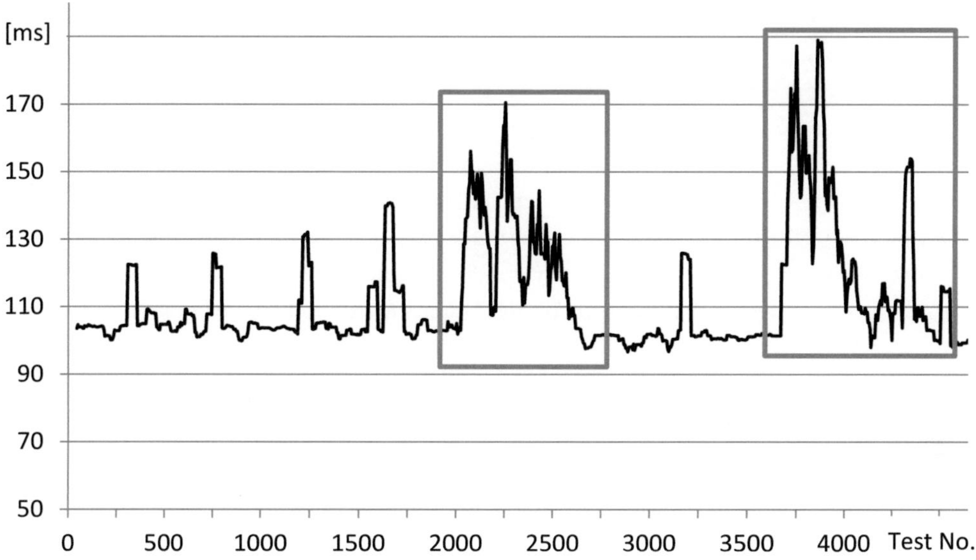

Figure 8.23.: Change of Staleness over Time (Cassandra, Multi-Region Setup)

requests were always routed to the closest replica. Cassandra clients were configured to use consistency level ONE for all requests[13].

During each test, we left the storage system at idle for at least 30 minutes before we started the actual consistency measurements. After another 30 minutes we then started YCSB running workload 1. When YCSB was done, we again waited for the storage system to stabilize before running workload 2. Finally, after completing workload 2, we asserted that the system stabilized again at the levels before each workload. This resulted in about 1000 to 1300 writes of the CMC per system benchmark run for which we measured our consistency metrics.

There were no cross effects between the three different tests as we started each storage system cluster from scratch. Both workloads comprised one million operations on 1000 records. Workload 1 had 80% reads and 20% writes, while workload 2 was configured exactly the other way around.

Results

Effects of Workload   Surprisingly, the workloads barely affected the inconsistency window (t-visibility) of both systems. We used Amazon CloudWatch[14] to also measure the CPU

---

[13]A request terminates successfully after having written or read a single replica.

[14]aws.amazon.com/cloudwatch

utilization and network IO of the replicas and the YCSB instance. In all cases, network IO of the "master" replica[15] seemed to be the bottleneck. During one system benchmark, while we were still testing the setup of our scripts, we managed to overload the CPU of Cassandra's "master" replica. During that period we observed very high staleness values. Obviously, when the CPU is saturated, the consistency behavior becomes completely unpredictable. Table 8.5 shows the CPU utilization that we encountered during our experiments.

During one of the tests (Cassandra in the multi-region setup), we were able to see an effect of the workloads on the inconsistency window. Figure 8.23 shows how staleness values changed over time during that experiment (the graph shows a moving average to remove extreme values). The boxes indicate the periods during which the two workloads were running.

Effects of Geo-Distribution For Cassandra, about 98% of all requests created an inconsistency window between zero and one millisecond when deployed within a single availability zone. As there was only a single maximum value of 38ms, we do not show a chart for this. For the setups where replicas were distributed over three availability zones or regions respectively, Figures 8.24 and 8.25 show the observed density functions for the inconsistency windows. We have excluded extreme values from our results to increase legibility of the chart. As expected, it is fairly obvious that increasing the level of geo-distribution increases staleness. We did not encounter any violations of MRC, MWC or RYWC which is caused by both the load balancing strategy that we chose (routing requests to the closest replica) as well as the fact that our system benchmarks did not encounter any obvious failures.

For MongoDB, the results were slightly different. As expected, the setup with replicas distributed over different regions showed the longest inconsistency window. We would have expected to see again a value of close to zero for the single availability zone setup and a slightly larger value for the setup in multiple availability zones. Interestingly though, this was exactly the other way around. See Figure 8.26 for the density functions of observed inconsistency windows on MongoDB.

When looking at the detailed results for the individual replicas[16], it becomes obvious that it was always the same replica that was lagging behind. When we excluded this replica, results are again as expected: More than 96% of all requests show an inconsistency window of 5ms or less in the single availability zone setup. We believe that this could be caused by one of two effects which are both related to problems with the respective virtual machine. Either the third replica had a problem (possibly due to a resource-greedy tenant on the same physical machine) and was really lagging behind or the reader for this replica had a clock synchronization issue which caused its clock to lag by around 10ms behind. Normally, this

---

[15]The load balancing strategy that we chose effectively asserted that all updates originated on the same replica.

[16]We do not report those detailed results here for reasons of legibility, but the CMC logs the result of every single datastore interaction as well as the corresponding timestamp and latency.

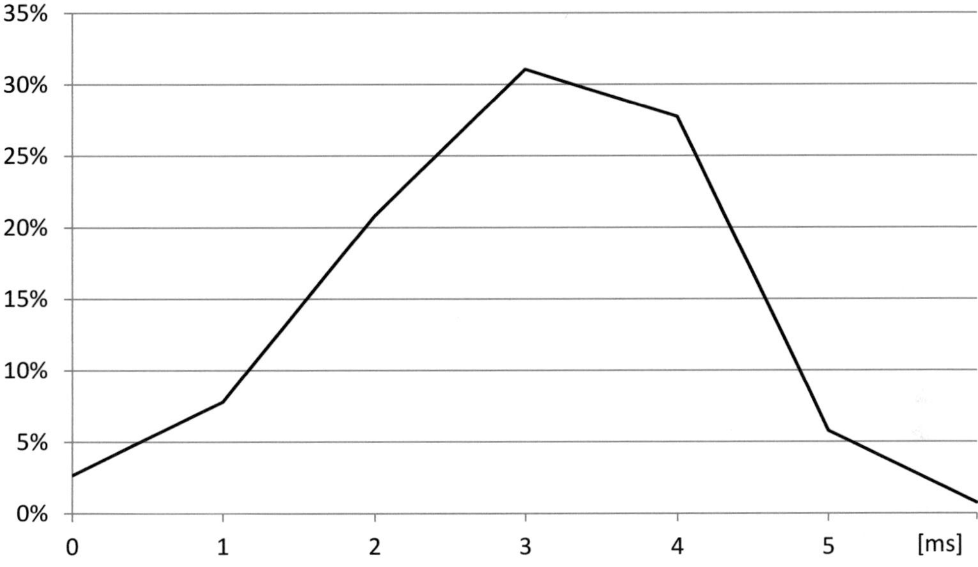

Figure 8.24.: Distribution of Staleness Values in Cassandra (Multi-AZ)

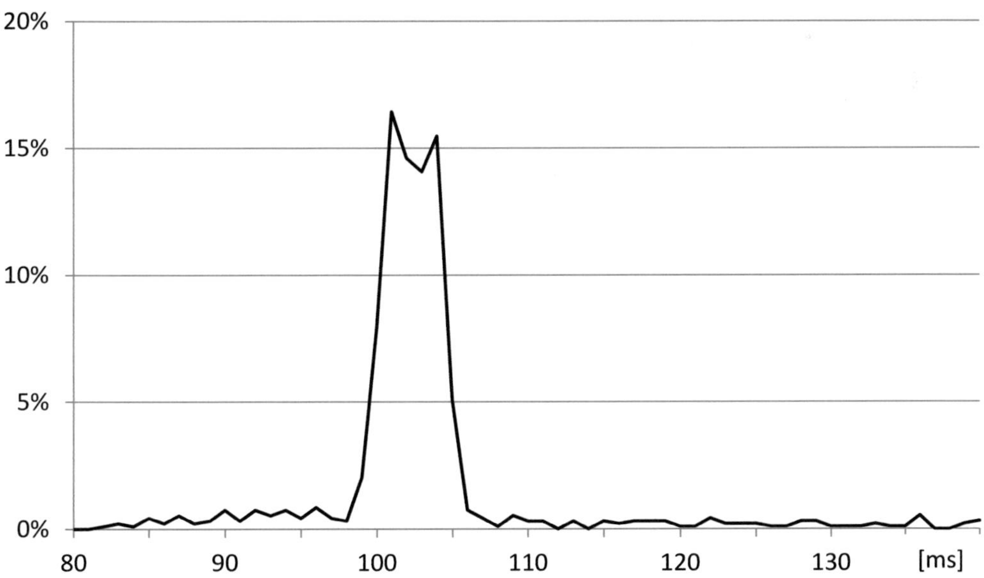

Figure 8.25.: Distribution of Staleness Values in Cassandra (Multi-Region)

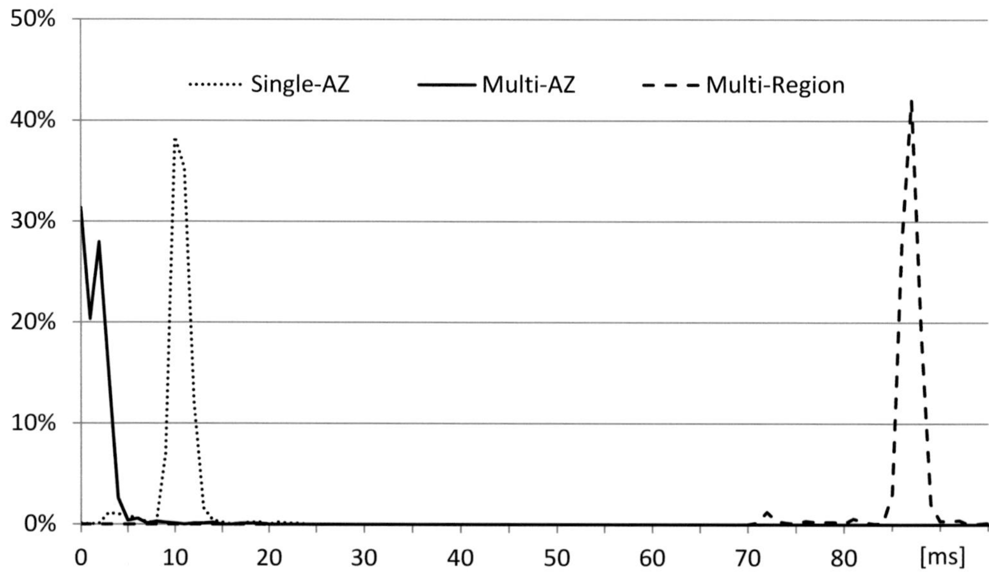

Figure 8.26.: Distribution of Staleness Values in MongoDB

should not be an issue as our CMC component was started about 24 hours in advance to allow for a slow clock synchronization process[17]. In this case, one possible reason for causing this effect is a problem with the virtual machine of the reader. However, further investigation is required to verify if other reasons could be behind this effect.

Again, we did not see any violations of MRC, MWC or RYWC due to the reasons outlined above.

During our multi-region tests with both Cassandra and MongoDB, we could observe that the Singapore region usually added another 15 to 20ms to the inconsistency window already caused by the us-west replica. Obviously, the connection to the Singapore replica was the limiting factor in our setup.

Additional Observations   For Cassandra, we also repeated a multi-region setup with a fourth replica in the region sao-paulo and varied the write consistency level of Cassandra which describes the number of replicas that need to acknowledge a write request so that it terminates successfully. In all of our tests, we could not see any variance in the staleness levels due to the write consistency level chosen. Obviously, the write consistency level is rather a durability level than a consistency level as the system does not block dirty reads. This implies that in a geo-distributed setting the updates might be visible on some replicas

---

[17]ntp.org recommends about 4 hours, so we really played it safe here.

before the request commits at the coordinator of the write which, in essence, corresponds to something like "negative staleness" according to our definitions from chapter 4. Apart from increased request latency there was no effect on the system.

8.3. Conclusion

In this chapter, we started with the evaluation of our consistency modeling and simulation approach and showed that our approach allows accurate predictions for data-centric staleness values. We also showed that for our other consistency metrics at least qualitatively correct predictions can be simulated.

Afterwards, we presented the results of a large number of experimental studies using our system benchmarking approach from chapter 6. First, we demonstrated that our client-centric system benchmarks in fact are a good approximation for actual behavior under the assumption that a sufficient number of readers is used. Our experiment also indicated that data-centric staleness is indeed an upper bound for client-centric staleness. Second, we conducted a long term experimental study of Amazon S3's consistency guarantees and revealed surprising changes in behavior. This, of course, also demonstrates the necessity of system benchmarks for client-centric consistency as a user of cloud storage services. Third, we studied how geo-replication and parallel workloads (i.e., changes in resource saturation) affect the consistency behavior of Apache Cassandra and MongoDB.

9. Application Engineering

Consistency Benchmarking not only serves the purpose of increasing comparability of storage systems or of allowing researchers to study consistency behavior for the identification of new mechanisms for improved future systems. It is also necessary for application developers who have to deal with inconsistencies of the storage system within their application. This is achieved by providing concrete insight into the frequency and severity of consistency violations – a necessity for efficient inconsistency handling. Without this information, handling conflicts is impossible for some kinds of inconsistency and highly inefficient for others.

Generally, consistency violations can be categorized in two groups: The first group comprises violations that can be handled independent of an actual application whereas the second group requires application-specific knowledge (e.g., when merging version branches). Middleware systems as both a programming abstraction and application infrastructure can be used to implement inconsistency handling for the first group, parts of which we presented at IC2E 2013 [16]. Doing this in an efficient way requires detailed knowledge on actual consistency behavior of an eventually consistent storage system.

Therefore, this chapter is divided into three sections:

- Section 9.1 describes for the example of a simple webshop how inconsistencies could generally be handled based on Consistency Benchmarking results. Since not all inconsistencies can be handled without application-specific knowledge, describing basic concepts and methods for inconsistency handling becomes much more comprehensible when done based on a use case instead of in terms of abstract concepts. For this reason, we describe such methods based on an exemplary use case and leave the development of abstract application engineering methods to future work.

- As already pointed out, some inconsistencies can be handled without application-specific knowledge, thus, reducing the complexity for application developers, e.g., the webshop provider, when implemented within a middleware layer. Section 9.2, therefore, generally describes how a middleware component running on the same machine as an application server can extend the eventually consistent guarantees of a storage system to also cover MRC and RYWC without making any changes to the storage system. This effectively guarantees that the storage system will appear to the application server as if it were offering CC, i.e., it creates the client-side illusion of CC by alleviating and hiding the effects of causal violations from the application server. This material is based on our IC2E 2013 publication [16].

- Section 9.3 describes how Consistency Benchmarking results can increase the efficiency of such a middleware system but also how applications can generally handle inconsistencies not requiring application-specific knowledge. Some of these inconsistency handling approaches would not be possible without our Consistency Benchmarking results – others can, this way, be used much more efficiently. We also describe potential extensions further increasing consistency guarantees which, though, partly interfere with other QoS levels like availability or latency.

Generally, applications running on top of NoSQL systems or cloud storage services always require a co-design of data store and application. Even apart from potential inconsistencies which, when not dealt with, will lead to unforeseeable, undesirable application behavior, applications need to be designed with the storage system in mind as there are no standard data structures and interfaces. Frequently, this is also works bidirectionally in that the data store is also designed for a specific application, e.g., Facebook's Cassandra [65]. While there are approaches working towards data store interoperability, e.g., DataNucleus[1], dealing with varying degrees of inconsistency is a complex problem which we aim to address in this chapter.

All in all, this chapter shall not only show how inconsistencies can be handled but also demonstrate how important Consistency Benchmarking is for application engineering on top of eventually consistent storage systems. Finally, we conclude this chapter with a conclusion in section 9.4.

9.1. Handling Inconsistencies in a Webshop Scenario

In the following, we use the example of a webshop to describe how inconsistencies can be handled in applications using application-specific information as well as Consistency Benchmarking results. Most effects from running an application on top of an only eventually consistent datastore can be mitigated by designing the application with the consistency behavior in mind instead of implementing it as if for running on top of an RDBMS. We describe this application design within this section.

Please note, that this example shall only illustrate how Consistency Benchmarking results can be used in inconsistency handling. Future work might develop an abstract application engineering method which, though, is beyond the scope of this work.

---

[1]datanucleus.org

We start with a scenario description in section 9.1.1 before discussing how inconsistencies can be handled for the various operations that interact with the eventually consistent storage system (section 9.1.2).

9.1.1. Scenario Description

Our scenario comprises two roles: a provider running a webshop on top of an eventually consistent storage system (i.e., multiple app servers which access the datastore[2]), and a number of customers who access the webshop, i.e., the app servers, via their browser. Employees of the provider also access the datastore for administrative tasks via their browser and an app server. For our purposes, we will assume that each of the roles has the following business operations which run on one ore more app servers at the provider and access the datastore directly:

- Provider operations
    - Changing product information or adding a new product.
    - Removing undesirable customer reviews.

- Customer operations
    - Searching for products.
    - Reading product details.
    - Writing product reviews.
    - Adding products to the shopping cart.
    - Check-out using the shopping cart.
    - Changing personal information of the customer (address, billing information, credentials, etc.).

9.1.2. Potential Conflicts and Resolution Mechanisms

In this section, we describe for each business operation how it might behave in the presence of inconsistencies as well as how it might affect other operations. Based on this, we then describe how the operation could be implemented to minimize the impact of inconsistencies visible to the customer. We start with the provider operations before continuing with the customer operations.

---

[2]We discuss a more abstract use case in section 9.2.

Provider Operations

Changing Product Information or Adding a New Product   For this operation, there
are five potential effects which can be caused by inconsistencies.

First, the employee changing information of a product or adding a new product might
not be able to see his own changes. This can be addressed by caching the updated value in
the employee's browser combined with vector clocks[3] or via employee education: why not
simply tell the employees that changes will not be visible everywhere right away?

Second, the amount on stock visible to a client may be wrong: Typically, a shop offers
only quantities for regular private households (for instance, a private household will rarely
buy more than one copy of the same book at the same time). So, while the amount on stock
is by comparison to these quantities large, inconsistencies are entirely uncritical as it does
not matter to a customer whether there are ten or a hundred copies left afterwards as long as
he is able to buy the desired quantity. For low values, the website could just show a warning
message that there are only a few items left. During the check-out process the system then
actually checks whether the item is available by using locking, by interacting with a larger
number of replicas or by communicating with a master replica only. This corresponds to the
approach also proposed as Consistency Rationing [60].

Third, the price changes during the check-out process which will lead to customer irritation. A cookie stored within the browser of the customer simply stores the version number of
the website and check-out always uses the version number which is specified by the cookie.
Whenever the price is changed, the old version is not overwritten but instead persisted under
a new version number. This way, customers will always get the price which they did see
when first accessing the product during the session. Values within the cookie expire, e.g.,
after a day, so that customers will not for eternity be able to buy the product for the old price.
If the expiration time is set to a day, it is also safe to delete the old version after a day plus a
safety margin for incorrect app server clocks.

Fourth, when a new product is added, the customer might not be able to find the product
information after selecting it from the search results when the search index is updated before
all replicas have been written[4]. Typically, no harm will be done if the new product is not
visible in searches right away. So, if the maximum staleness duration T is known, then the
search index could be updated T after inserting the new product into the storage system.

Fifth, the description of the product changes during the check-out process so that a customer in the end receives something different than what he ordered. This can be avoided by
treating all product description updates like the insertion of a new product into the database:
The new description is persisted under a different key so that even a reload of the website

---

[3]This corresponds to the approach also taken in our middleware component, cf. section 9.2.
[4]In PNUTS[32], this is called "timeline consistency" which is actually CC.

will return the old description. The amount on stock can then be set to zero so that, during the check-out process, the customer can be notified that the product is no longer available but that there is a similar product or a new version of his selection.

Removing Undesirable Content   Deleting data like customer reviews or comments usually happens for a reason, hence, an undesirable effect would be that the review can be seen by parts of the customer after deletion has been triggered. If time is not critical, this is unproblematic, but frequently the reputation of the provider is endangered if this effect takes too long. Still, if there are multiple replicas and potentially even additional copies in caching layers, then there is no way around removing all these copies as fast as possible, i.e., to minimize the time during which the respective data is still visible to the customer. For this reason, we propose to just broadcast the delete request to all replicas (i.e., not to rely on update propagation of the storage system) and to issue explicit cache invalidations as well. This, of course, requires implementing such a delete operation in an idempotent way.

As we have seen in our experiments, actual staleness values tend to be well below one minute, i.e., the time necessary for an employee to be notified of such a review, to read it and to decide whether to delete it or not far exceeds the potential staleness in the absence of failures. The only problematic case will, thus, be if a replica which stores the data fails before receiving the delete request, comes online again much later and continues to return the data. This could, for instance, be addressed by sending some kind of warning to the load balancer(s) between the app servers and the storage system not to accept responses from the respective replica unless told that this is safe again. The machine originating the delete requests would then be responsible to notify the failed machine as well as the load balancers when the failed replica is up-to-date again. Other machines might help with this task in case the original machines fails at well.

Customer Operations

Searching for Products   If the search index is replicated and customers read from different replicas, then MRC might be violated, i.e., when repeating a search, products from the last result set might suddenly vanish or new ones might appear. The easiest way to address this is to use sticky sessions both for the connection between app servers and replicas as well as for the connection between clients and app servers – at least for subsequent searches for the same search terms. In the few cases where this does not work due to failed replicas or app servers, the consequences will not be severe as customers will likely expect the webshop to continuously update its product portfolio.

Reading Product Details   We already outlined several potential problems in our provider operations above (e.g., not being able to access an item found via search). Beyond these, we recommend to persist the entire product information and reviews under the same key so that they are replicated as one entity. This helps to remove problems where, for instance, a product review refers to another product review which is not included in the returned version. If such a problem occurs, vector clocks could be used as metadata to identify a version history. As conflicts are unlikely to be noticed by the customer right away, AJAX might be used to refetch the missing items in the background so that the temporary conflict is hidden.

Writing Product Reviews   For the writing of product reviews, there are two potential problems: Edits of a customer might be lost completely due to violations of MWC or a customer will not be able to see his own review during a subsequent access. The first issue, in case MWC is not guaranteed – which is rare, can be addressed by never overwriting existing reviews but instead persisting it under a separate key or in a separate column for table-oriented datastores. By adding vector clocks or simple version numbers, app servers can then exclude the old version if the new one can be found as well within the returned data set. When all replicas have acknowledged writing the new version, the old version can simply be deleted to save disk space or be left behind if a version history is of interest. Of course, if MWC is guaranteed, this issue will not occur.

The second issue, where a customer is not able to see his own review during a subsequent read, can be addressed by notifying the customer after submitting his review that "it will shortly be visible" or that "it has been recorded". Potentially, such a message might even hint at a (fictional) content moderation by employees depending on the maximum staleness values as well as probability of RYWC violations. This mechanism falls in the category of user education.

Adding Items to the Shopping Cart   In this operation, potential issues involve lost updates by the client or the client not being able to see his own updates and the results of previous reads. If MWC, MRC and RYWC are guaranteed, this cannot occur. If not, the easiest approach is to keep a master copy of the shopping cart in a cookie at the client and to use the storage system as backup only. This way, the client will always see changes right away, updates are unlikely to be lost and the response time for user interaction is very low as well. The shopping cart could then just be sent with every request (ID and quantity of products are not too much data – especially when using compact encodings or compression). Optionally, the app server might also verify and, if necessary, reissue an update after the observed maximum staleness value plus a safety margin.

An alternative approach for this is taken in Amazon's Dynamo [37].

Check-out Using the Shopping Cart For the check-out operation, several issues are possible: First, the order recorded in the storage system might not reflect what the customer perceives to be his order. Second, a product might not longer be available. Third, the price might have changed.

For the last two issues, we have already described how they can be addressed. The first issue, though, is already partly addressed by our "add to shopping cart" operation: By keeping a master copy at the client and using this master copy (instead of a version from the storage system) to create an order object under a new key, it is asserted that both perspectives will be identical. If, afterwards, access to the order object is read-only, then no discrepancies can occur.

Changing Personal Information Changing personal information is often critical, for instance, when changing the shipping address, the billing information or the user credentials. The first two cases can be addressed by caching that information at the client as well and using it within a potential new order object (same approach as with the shopping cart: keeping the master copy at the client). A background process can then verify later that all replicas have been written correctly.

User credentials are not as critical: Updates may not be lost but there is typically no time limitation until when the update needs to be applied since a customer is unlikely to log off and then log in again directly afterwards. Furthermore, user education could again help in this case: By telling a user that it might take a little while until his changes have been applied the customer will not be as irritated if he cannot re-login directly afterwards. Furthermore, staleness values are typically very small so that the time interval where problems might occur is rather small as well.

If MWC is not guaranteed, i.e., there is a chance that the update is lost, then mechanisms which we outline in section 9.3.2 can be used to address this problem. Alternatively, if stronger consistency levels are supported as well, changing personal information is a good candidate for using them. See also [60], who argue in the same direction.

9.2. A Middleware Guaranteeing Client-centric Consistency

As already discussed, handling inconsistencies within applications is possible but burdens application developers with additional complexity. For this purpose, it is desirable to handle all inconsistencies not requiring application-specific knowledge within a middleware layer. For instance, some of the approaches described in our use case above are only necessary if MRC and RYWC are not guaranteed by a storage system. If a middleware running between application and storage system can add those two guarantees, then complexity is shifted from the application developer to the middleware. In this section, we, therefore, describe how a middleware component running on the same machine as an application server can guarantee MRC and RYWC for said application server.

Before we can describe our approach, though, we have to clarify the definitions of both guarantees first: Both guarantees require that the result of a read operation reflects the results of all previous read (MRC) respectively write (RYWC) operations by the same application server. This is obviously fulfilled if the returned version is identical or newer to the last one seen respectively written. In cases where multiple competing versions are returned this is not as clear, as the requirement could be that the condition is fulfilled either for *at least one* returned value (existential quantor, $\exists$) or for *all* returned values (universal quantor, $\forall$). For our purposes, we believe that the existential quantor suffices since all necessary information is captured, i.e.,

- MRC is fulfilled if the result set of a read following a read of version n contains at least one version $\geq n$;

- RYWC is fulfilled if the result set of a read following a write of version n contains at least one version $\geq n$.

This way, even version branches having occurred before the last datastore interaction may be seen in a read operation. Otherwise, such an entirely valid version would have to be excluded from the results or automatically merged. We, therefore, believe that our definition using the existential quantor is the most pragmatic definition.

Beyond this definition, our approach includes several roles apart from the storage system (see figure 9.1 for a high level overview of the scenario we want to address):

1. *App server*: An application with consistency requirements beyond those guaranteed by the storage system is running on one or more machines. A single server running application code is called an app server. App servers do not need to interact directly but may of course do so.

2. *Middleware*: The middleware service which we propose is currently implemented as a Java library which can be used directly within an application. Each app server uses its own middleware instance running on the same machine. Middleware instances do not need to communicate with other middleware instances. All app server requests to the storage system are routed via the middleware.

3. *End user*: An end user usually uses a software client (e.g., a browser) to interact with one app server instance. This software client is running on a different machine than all app servers or the storage system. To avoid confusion, we use the term *end user* for the combination of the software client and the underlying physical device the software client is running on.

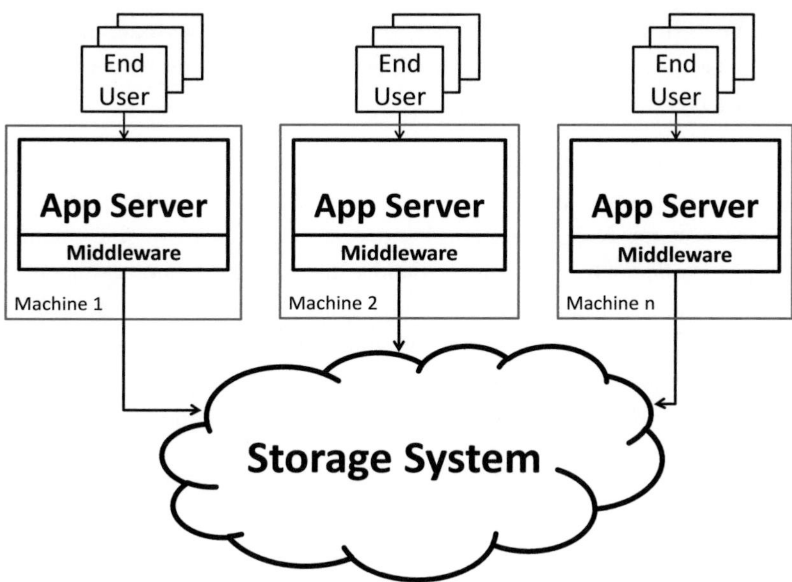

Figure 9.1.: Intended Use Case

As an example setup, Amazon S3[5] could be used as the storage system. The app servers could be distributed over multiple compute services and on-premises servers running a standard web application (e.g., an internet forum or a webshop). End users of said web application might access the web application via browsers on their desktop computers or mobile devices.

Vector clocks [40] are a well known mechanism to capture causality. In the context of eventually consistent distributed storage systems, they can be used to describe a version history like, e.g., in Amazon Dynamo [37]. Whenever conflicting versions exist on some replica, it is then possible to resolve all conflicts automatically that were not caused by concurrent updates (e.g., conflicts caused by update propagation delays or fail-recover errors).

Our approach uses vector clocks to identify (a) which version was last *seen* by a particular app server and (b) which version was last *written* by a particular app server. This allows to create a total order for all writes by the same app server (a prerequisite for MWC and WFRC) and for writes that update another app server's write upon reading it (a prerequisite for CC). It also allows to check whether MRC and RYWC are violated or not. The data itself and the corresponding vector clock metadata are persisted under the same key.

---

[5]aws.amazon.com/s3

Now, as some inconsistencies can be identified, the app server at least knows about them. This leaves the issue of dealing with them which we propose to do via client-side caching, i.e., on the app server.

- Whenever an app server requests a datum from the storage system, the middleware reads from the storage system and adds a copy of that datum to its local cache if the cache does not already contain that datum in that exact version (identified by its vector clock). Older versions superseded by the data read from the storage system are replaced in the cache and all conflicting versions are returned to the app server. The app server is then expected to merge conflicting versions (this could even be dropping all but one version) at application level considering the semantics of the data. This conflict resolution scheme is similar to the approach taken in Amazon Dynamo [37].

- Whenever an app server requests a write following a read, the middleware assigns a vector clock value that supersedes all cached values of that datum and writes it to the storage system. Afterwards, the middleware replaces all cached versions with the value and vector clock it just wrote to the storage system.

- Whenever an app server spontaneously writes a value, the middleware assigns a vector clock that is in conflict with all cached values to guarantee that no versions are lost due to this concurrent update. It then adds the data to the local cache and writes it to the storage system.

- Storage systems guaranteeing CC, typically capture only internal causality but not external causality [90] where a client of the storage system gets to know a new version not via the storage system but rather using external means of communication with another client. To also capture external causality, the middleware offers a notification feature which allows the app server to update the cache directly. As long as the app server uses this feature whenever he gets knowledge of an update using external means of communication, the middleware guarantees to capture external causality as well.

Our approach guarantees MRC and RYWC and creates the client-side (i.e., at the app server) illusion of per key CC[6] as so-called session consistency, i.e., guarantees exist for the duration of a session but not beyond. A session is initiated by an app server and ends either if the app server terminates the session, if the app server fails or if the cache fails. Furthermore, while a middleware outside of the storage system cannot guarantee MWC[7] it certainly helps towards that goal by reissuing "all" writes in correct order with every update,

---

[6]We cannot actually guarantee CC without having control over the storage system itself, but to the app server our middleware guarantees the same behavior as the storage system would do if it offered CC.

[7]It cannot affect the behavior of the storage system which may just decide to drop arbitrary updates.

thus, increasing the probability of correct serialization within the storage system. The same holds true for WFRC.

Commercial cloud storage offerings typically return only one version, using a last write wins strategy internally. This can result in potentially many lost updates based on the rate of concurrent updates. Our approach avoids this completely as long as there is for every update at least one session which holds that update within its local cache.

9.2.1. Overhead and Intended Use Case

Our approach adds some overheads: First, there is a storage overhead for persisting the vector clocks within the storage system (which will typically create additional cost for cloud storage systems). Second, there is a compute overhead involved for every read as at least two vector clocks need to be compared. Third, there is another (local) storage overhead for keeping a persistent local cache.

The first overhead for persisting the vector clocks is negligible for most scenarios. A vector clock containing 100 entries, for example, requires less than 500 Bytes in its current (not very efficient) implementation. The size could be further reduced using, e.g., compression.

The second overhead for comparing vector clocks directly depends on the number of entries in the respective vector clocks. Therefore, it is desirable to keep the number of app servers relatively small – since a typical app server should be able to handle hundreds or thousands of end users in parallel, the number of app servers is small compared to the number of end users served. With today's server's computing power, the second overhead should, hence, not become an issue. Furthermore, the size of the vector clock does not directly depend on the number of app servers involved but on the number of app servers issuing writes. Hence, read-heavy workloads should not create any problem at all while for write-heavy workloads there could be mechanisms like routing updates for a certain key always via the same app server to further reduce the number of vector clock entries.

In our intended use case, the third overhead (storage cost of the local cache) does not really matter: A set of independent app servers interacts with a storage system using our middleware. As app servers typically do not persist data locally (apart from log files), the local hard disk drive should be more or less unused and can, hence, be used for a local cache without or with little side effects. Furthermore, there is a relation between the update frequency and the size of a datum: Small files are usually updated frequently while very large files are mostly write-once data. Thus, the third overhead of keeping a persistent local cache should become negligible as well as only small files need to be cached.

Even though the decision might be different for different applications, we believe that typically the consistency benefits far outweigh the overheads incurred. Our approach is especially helpful, if there is a huge number of concurrent requests to only a few keys with small data items. The smaller the size and number of the data items, the more feasible is our approach. If there are only a few concurrent updates, the feasibility of using our approach depends on whether the data store guarantees MRC. To our knowledge, no cloud storage service or production-ready open source system exists that can give these guarantees. So, we believe it is safe to say that any scenario where data items are updated from time to time (instead of being written only once), can benefit from using our approach.

9.2.2. Handling Sessions

From a QoS perspective, the consistency guarantees of the middleware should be extended to the end user as he is the one who will be irritated if unread emails vanish, he cannot read the blog comment he just posted and so on. At the same time, the local cache might grow over time as more and more data items from the storage system are accessed by the end users. Also, conflicting versions need additional space. To limit the size of the local cache, we propose the following approach to session handling:

1. Start a middleware session on the app server.

2. Accept end user requests and hold sessions with them using standard session management features of the app server.

3. When the local cache has grown too much, restart from step 1 and accept new end user sessions only within the scope of the new session.

4. Terminate the old middleware session as soon as all end user sessions of the old app server session have completed.

When the main goal is avoiding lost updates, then another strategy would be to drop items from the cache as soon as an update to the respective app server's write has been read by that same app server. This works because reading an update guarantees that another app server has included the own value in its cache. Of course, while this avoids lost updates and keeps the cache small, it does not address MRC or RYWC.

9.2.3. Consistency Guarantees

We show that the usage of the provided middleware guarantees the same client-centric consistency levels as a storage system that implements CC. In the following, C_i stands for app server number i. This is without loss of generality as the same guarantees hold for any client of a storage system using our middleware.

Definition: Operations. *Let O_{Li} denote the set of operations of a middleware L_i. We refer to the operations themselves as:*

- $w_i(x)v$ - *request of C_i to perform a write operation under key x and value v.*

- $r_i(x)v$ - *request of C_i to perform a read operation under key x and value v.*

- $o_i(x)v$ *request of C_i to perform any operation under key x and value v.*

Definition: Vector Clocks. *We refer to the vector clock of an operation $o_i(x)v$ as $vc(o_i(x)v) \in VC$ where VC denotes the set of vector clocks visible to a single middleware instance. The binary relation $<$ imposes a linear order on the set VC. We call $<$ the data-centric view order.*

Definition: App server's View Order. *The binary relation $\overset{C_i}{\mapsto}$ orders the views on results of write operation for an app server C_i. We refer to $\mapsto$ as app server's view order.*

THEOREM 1. *The middleware shows exactly the same behavior as a storage system that guarantees CC.*

Proof. Causal consistency requires that the view order of a client (in our case of an app server) on operations follows the causal order of operations [23]. An operation $o1$ causally precedes an operation $o2$ ($o1 \rightsquigarrow o2$) if one of the following conditions hold [23, 5]:

$$\exists_{C_j}(o_1 \overset{C_j}{\rightarrow} o_2) \tag{9.1}$$

$$o_1 = w(x)v \wedge o_2 = r(x)v \tag{9.2}$$

$$\exists_{o \in O}(o_1 \rightsquigarrow o \wedge o \rightsquigarrow o_2) \tag{9.3}$$

I.e., either both operations were issued by the same client, or $o2$ was a read operation which returned the value of the write operation $o1$, or there was an other operation o which created a transitive relation between $o1$ and $o2$ using one of the first two conditions.

We use the notation $o_a \rightsquigarrow o_b|(9.1)$ to denote that operation o_a causally precedes operation o_b according to conditions (9.1) - (9.3). At the client-side, a storage system guarantees CC if the following condition is preserved [23]:

$$\forall_{C_i} \forall_{o_1,o_2 \in OW \cup OC_i} \left(o_1 \rightsquigarrow o_2 \Rightarrow o_1 \overset{C_i}{\mapsto} o_2 \right) \tag{9.4}$$

It is necessary to show that the middleware provides a causally consistent view on operations for all app servers according to (9.4). Consequently, we consider the different conditions for causal ordering (9.1) - (9.3).

1. We show that a causally consistent view is preserved if two operations are of causal order according to (9.1).

Proof. We assume that an app server C_j requests two consecutive write operations $w(x)a$ and $w(x)b$ for key x: $w(x)a \xrightarrow{C_j} w(x)b$. By contradiction, we assume that an app server C_i exists that views the result of $w(x)a$ after the result of $w(x)b$: $w(x)b \xmapsto{C_i} w(x)a$. We consider the two cases that the middleware reads $w(x)a$ from the cache and remote storage after reading $w(x)b$.

a) We assume the cache returns the result of $w(x)a$. In order for the local cache to return the result of $w(x)a$ after the result of $w(x)b$, the following condition must hold: $vc(w(x)b) < vc(w(x)a)$ which leads to contradiction because of $w(x)a \xrightarrow{C_j} w(x)b$ which implies $vc(w(x)a) < vc(w(x)b)$.

b) We assume the remote storage returns the result of $w(x)a$. The assumption that the cache returns the result of $w(x)a$ leads to contradiction according to 1a). We assume that the cache returns the result of $w(x)b$ while the middleware returns the result of $w(x)a$. This implies $vc(w(x)b) < vc(w(x)a)$ which leads to contradiction according to 1a).

$\square$

2. A causally consistent view is preserved for C_i if $o_1 \rightsquigarrow o_2$ according to (9.2).

Proof. As the read does not change the state, the results of both o_1 and o_2 are identical. Hence, the app server's view order can never be violated.

$\square$

3. A causally consistent view is preserved for C_i if $o_1 \rightsquigarrow o_2$ according to (9.3).

Proof. Transitivity of the causally precedes relation $\rightsquigarrow$ is generally guaranteed by the linear ordering of the ordering relation $<$ over the set of vector clocks VC. For the sake of completeness, we conduct the proof as follows:

We assume that an operation o_1 precedes an operation o according to condition (9.1) or (9.2). Furthermore, we assume operation o precedes operation o_2 according to condition (9.1) or (9.2). By contradiction we assume: $o_2 \xmapsto{C_i} o_1$. Therefore, four different cases should satisfy the condition (9.3) based on the assumptions made.

a) $o_1 \rightsquigarrow o|(9.1) \wedge o \rightsquigarrow o_2|(9.1)$, i.e., all operations are writes by the same app server: This case leads to contradiction according to the proof of (1) as the $<$ relation on the vector clocks is transitive itself.

b) $o_1 \rightsquigarrow o|(9.1) \wedge o \rightsquigarrow o_2|(9.2)$, i.e., o_1 and o are writes by the same app server, o_2 is a read by another app server: According to the proof of (2), o and o_2 have the same result which leads to contradiction according to the proof of (1).

c) $o_1 \rightsquigarrow o|(9.2) \wedge o \rightsquigarrow o_2|(9.1)$, i.e. o_1 is a write and o and o_2 are a read and a write by another app server:

   We assume C_j orders a write operation $w(x)a$ and any app server C_k views the result of the write operation $w(x)a$ before updating the value with $w(x)b$, i.e., $\exists_{C_j} w(x)a \wedge \exists_{C_k} r(x)a \xrightarrow{C_k} w(x)b$. We assume by contradiction that an app server C_n exists that views the result of $w(x)a$ after the result of $w(x)b$: $w(x)b \xmapsto{C_n} w(x)a$.

   We consider the two cases that the middleware views the result of $w(x)a$ from the cache and remote storage after returning the result of $w(x)b$ to any client C_n.

   i. We assume the cache returns the result of $w(x)a$. Since C_n has already seen the result of $w(x)b$ (either because he issued $w(x)b$ or because he read the result of $w(x)b$), the cache contains the result of $w(x)b$ and must return $w(x)b$ as $vc(w(x)a) < vc(w(x)b)$. This leads to contradiction.

   ii. We assume the remote storage returns the result of $w(x)a$: According to 3c)i, the cache returns $w(x)b$. Because $vc(w(x)a) < vc(w(x)b)$, the middleware always returns $w(x)b$ which contradicts the original assumption of $w(x)b \xmapsto{C_n} w(x)a$.

d) $o_1 \rightsquigarrow o|(9.2) \wedge o \rightsquigarrow o_2|(9.2)$: This case leads to contradiction according to the proof of (2) as o would have to be a write and a read at the same time which is not possible.

$\square$

$\square$

9.2.4. Implementation

Our middleware has been prototypically implemented as a Java 6 library. Users can start one or more sessions with the same or different storage systems, each using its own local cache which is persistently written to disk. This is done via the `ConsistencyManager` singleton. Within the scope of a session, it is then possible to interact with cache and data stores using an adapter framework which offers operations to read, write and delete data items. Currently, adapters exist for the Amazon services S3[8], DynamoDB[9] and SimpleDB[10]

---

[8] aws.amzon.com/s3
[9] aws.amzon.com/dynamodb
[10] aws.amzon.com/simpledb

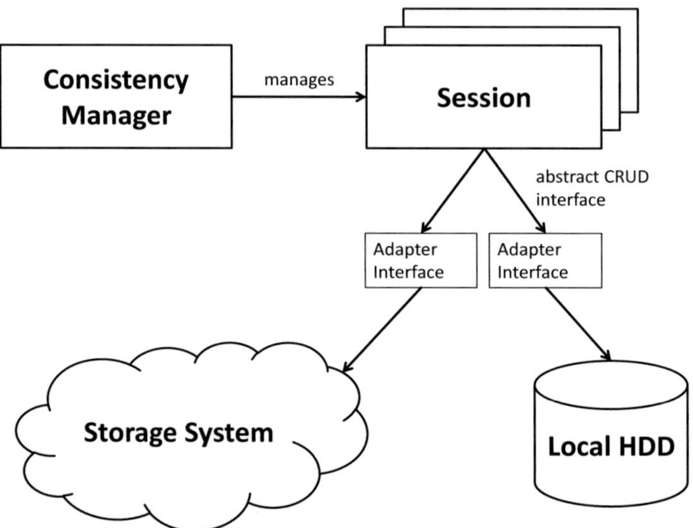

Figure 9.2.: Basic Middleware Architecture

– additional adapters just have to implement an interface and specify a mapping of multi-dimensional keys to the underlying data store. Figure 9.2 shows a high-level overview of the library's architecture.

Whenever a session is terminated (either directly by the user or indirectly via a crash of one or more components), the cache on the local disk is removed.

9.2.5. Evaluation

While we have formally shown that our approach is correct, we also wanted to test our middleware. We, therefore, first implemented and used a simulation environment to verify that our approach works under adverse conditions. Afterwards, we switched to experiments with a sample application running on top of several cloud storage offerings to also demonstrate the importance of using our middleware approach.

Simulation

A special storage adapter (see section 9.2.4) randomly drops updates and returns arbitrary values. We used it in a configuration where it created violations of MRC and RYWC for about 50% of all requests to really strain our middleware implementation (commercial cloud storage offerings usually offer lower rates of violations, e.g., see the results from chapter 8).

Next, we implemented a test application, which just reads and writes random values and checks each time for MRC and RYWC violations, and used it with this adapter.

During several billion simulated requests each, we never encountered any consistency violations as long as our middleware was used. When running the same setup without our middleware, we could observe the expected number of inconsistencies.

Sample Application

As our sample application, we chose an internet forum as this allows to easily check for inconsistencies. We believe, though, that any other application would show the same or comparable results. Our internet forum implementation had ten conversation threads. During every test run clients would randomly choose one, read it completely, add a response and write it back as well as check for violations of MRC or RYWC. Each system benchmark was repeated several times and used 30 clients which were deployed on 30 EC2[11] micro instances in the region eu-west, ten per availability zone. Each client executed 1,000 test runs, thus, totalling a number of 30,000 reads and writes each per system benchmark. We ran system benchmarks with and without our middleware for S3, DynamoDB (consistent and eventually consistent reads) and SimpleDB (also consistent and eventually consistent reads). Whenever we incurred an availability error, the system benchmark just repeated the respective test run until it completed successfully. Each test configuration (e.g., DynamoDB with middleware and consistent reads) was repeated several times.

Results

As expected, all test runs using our middleware showed no violations of MRC and RYWC. When not using the middleware, i.e., accessing the data store directly, we could see enormous numbers of consistency violations. Figures 9.3 and 9.4 show box plots of the number of consistency violations incurred by our 30 clients (CR stands for consistent read, ER stands for eventually consistent read). A value of 500 means that out of 1,000 reads half were consistency violations. Results for each test configuration were relatively stable when rerunning our system benchmarks, i.e., the standard deviation values of repeated tests within one test configuration were close to zero.

Apart from counting inconsistencies, we also measured latencies for reads and writes to determine whether there is any relevant latency overhead caused by our middleware. During several S3 system benchmarks, we did not see any deviations – neither between different system benchmarks nor depending on using the middleware or not. Based on that, we believe

---

[11]aws.amazon.com/ec2

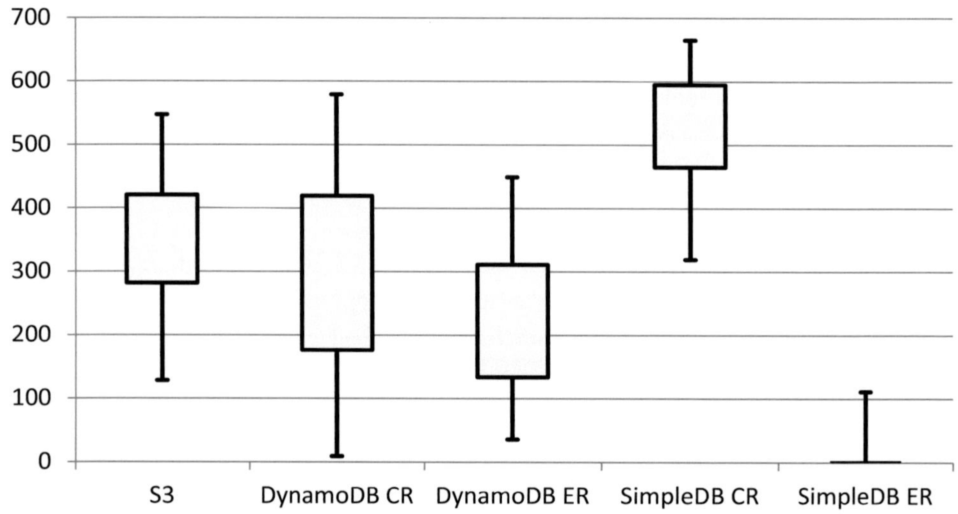

Figure 9.3.: Violations of MRC without Middleware

it is feasible to say that the latency overhead caused by our middleware is negligible. In fact, values with middleware were often a little less than without middleware.

In our DynamoDB and SimpleDB system benchmarks we saw extensive variability (between a few hundred and several thousand milliseconds) in the latency values as well as a large number of availability issues – both for test runs with and without middleware. This could either be due to general problems of the service at the time of our test run or due to creating too much load[12]. We could neither see arguments in favor of or against a latency overhead of our middleware during those tests as it was just not possible to identify a statistically relevant result.

Discussion

When comparing our results to the system benchmarking results from chapter 8, it seems that the number of violations of RYWC depends on the number of concurrent updates as well as the update propagation speed of the data store which often implements a last write wins strategy: If the update propagation is too slow, the value will be overwritten by the next update. If there are only a few concurrent updates, there is more time to propagate the

---

[12]In [58], Kossmann et al. discovered that several cloud storage systems, including SimpleDB, scale very poorly. For S3, in contrast, they could not find any scalability limitations.

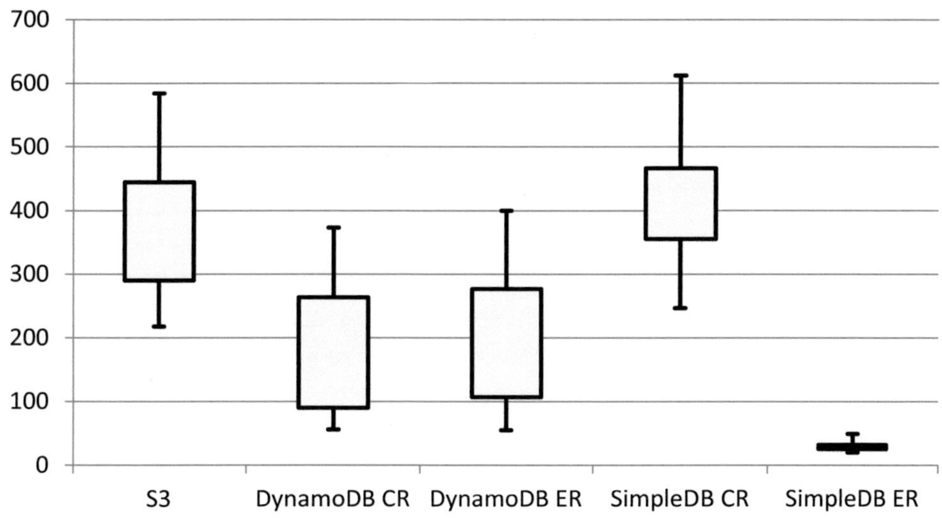

Figure 9.4.: Violations of RYWC without Middleware

update. The number of MRC violations, in contrast, depends more on the rate of updates than its origin plus the degree of session stickiness offered by a system.

Both the MRC and RYWC results for SimpleDB are interesting in that matter as they hint that a consistent read contains the newest value written which just might be a concurrent update. The eventually consistent read, in contrast, is likely to read the same replica which the client interacted with before, i.e., a high degree of session stickiness. This can also be seen in the MRC results for DynamoDB, though, definitely less pronounced.

Our evaluation clearly shows that especially applications with large numbers of concurrent updates benefit from using our approach. Our system benchmarking results from chapter 8 show that even when this is not the case, consistency violations occur at least from time to time and applications must be able to cope with it. Often this will mean implementing some variant of our approach at application level, e.g., by reloading data whenever a violation is detected [21].

Based on our results, we believe it is a better idea to handle such violations at the middleware level, i.e., in our case by using our middleware, than at either application level or within the storage system.

A downside of our approach is an overhead both in terms of cost and time for persistence, network transfer and comparison of the vector clocks. For our test application, this overhead was negligible. It would be interesting to see, though, how this changes for different applications and workload – especially, when considering worst case applications with very large numbers of app servers issuing a very high write load and, thus, creating vector clocks with many entries as well as many conflicting versions. A detailed analysis of this is beyond the scope of this work.

9.3. Efficient Inconsistency Handling

As we have seen in section 9.2, client-side caching combined with vector clocks as metadata can create the client-side illusion of CC, i.e., guarantee MRC and RYWC. This approach, though, adds an overhead which makes it not feasible for all use cases. For instance, data is cached for the duration of a session. If over the course of a session a large number of keys is accessed by the respective client, then our middleware component will essentially create a local copy of the data for all these keys – potentially even for all keys. Depending on the available disk space on a an app server this limits the maximum duration of sessions and, thus, indirectly the applicability as guarantees can only be provided within a session.

In this section, we, therefore, both introduce extensions which provide additional guarantees beyond MRC and RYWC, as well as show up modifications which provide almost the same guarantees in a much more efficient way accepting only very low levels of uncertainty.

9.3.1. Modifications to Increase Efficiency

If Consistency Benchmarking has identified the distribution of t-Visibility values, i.e., the probability of each (maximum) staleness value is known, then there is trade-off between the caching duration and the probability of violations after a value has been purged from the cache. For instance, if there is an 80% chance of t-Visibility being lower than 5 seconds and an 80% chance of not violating MRC suffices, then results of previous reads need only be cached for 5 seconds. Almost the same guarantees as our original middleware approach can, obviously, be achieved if data is cached for the duration of the maximum t-Visibility value and if an additional read has verified that the value is actually returned after that time. Still, there is a small degree of uncertainty left that a random staleness peak, e.g., caused by failures, violates these guarantees. Based on the business use case on top of the middleware component, it can be decided if this risk is acceptable or not. Using mechanisms like Consistency Rationing [60], it might also make sense to use different strategies for different kinds of data.

Another approach for scenarios where the knowledge whether MRC and RYWC are fulfilled suffices would be to cache vector clocks only as proposed by [21]. This will typically reduce the storage overhead for caching significantly and still guarantee that all violations will be noticed. Also, depending on the concrete requirements of the use case it might be acceptable to remove our middleware altogether for small staleness values or low probabilities of MRC and RYWC violations.

Generally, Consistency Benchmarking results provide the necessary input for an informed decision regarding the use of mechanisms for inconsistency handling based on fact instead of speculation.

9.3.2. Extensions for Additional Guarantees

MWC can be guaranteed in combination with our caching approach by periodically reading a value to assert that the serialization order is correct and (if necessary) reissuing the second update. As we have seen in system benchmarks, MWC is often guaranteed without being specified as part of an SLA. In those cases, the overhead for the MWC verification can be omitted if Consistency Benchmarking has identified that MWC is guaranteed. A more efficient implementation could set the periodicity for verification as slightly larger than the maximum observed staleness value so that both updates should have reached all replicas. In the absence of byzantine failures, this should guarantee MWC if the verification read returns the value of the second update.

If there are several clients, each running our middleware component and the application requires lower staleness values than the storage system offers (as determined by Consistency Benchmarking), then one possible solution is to "CC" the other app server's middleware component comparable to within an email, i.e., notify the other middleware component of the update and its value. The lowest achievable staleness value in that case is the one-way latency for sending the update to the other app server. This also explicitly captures external causality as described in section 9.2.

This could even be continued further: If our middleware components either run some kind of agreement algorithm, e.g., Paxos [67, 68], or distribute the responsibility for key ranges among the middleware instances by routing requests for a certain key always via the respective app server's middleware instance, then our approach could even guarantee SC. Since this affects latency and availability of the storage system (or rather blocks requests within the middleware layer), a fallback solution coupled with timeouts could be to use the existing approach, i.e., try to achieve SC but fall back to CC if this is not possible. This would also expose the trade-offs of the CAP theorem and PACELC model in a very transparent way: response times and availability of the storage system versus the frequency of only causally consistent datastore access.

An alternative approach which still keeps the positive properties of CC[13] while providing the illusion of SC to the client would be to specify a rule according to which all conflicting

---

[13]CC is the strongest consistency level which can be achieved when all replicas shall always be able to accept updates [72].

vector clocks of version branches will be merged in the very same deterministic way as well as a set of rules for merging arbitrary conflicting versions in a deterministic way as well. Since this guarantees that all middleware components would order all writes deterministically in the same total order, the middleware system alone would then guarantee SC. If an eventually consistent storage system is used for durability at least the client-side illusion of SC can be achieved while maintaining the availability properties of CC since all conflicts can be resolved locally and in a decentralized way. Obviously, the rule set for merging of version branches requires application-specific knowledge – an approach taken with the conflict resolvers in the Ficus File System [83].

9.4. Conclusion

In this chapter, we have discussed how applications can generally handle inconsistencies, preferably based on Consistency Benchmarking results. We also demonstrated how middleware components can increase the consistency guarantees of an eventually consistent storage system as well as how Consistency Benchmarking results can be used to increase the efficiency such a solution.

For this purpose, we started with the presentation of an application use case in section 9.1 – we chose the webshop scenario already introduced in chapter 1. In this use case, we identified several business operations which interact with the datastore and described in detail how an implementation might look like that keeps the aspect of consistency issues in mind in contrast to more conventional implementations running on top of strictly consistent databases. We also pointed out how the implementation might differ depending on client-centric consistency guarantees of the datastore.

Some inconsistencies can be resolved without application-specific knowledge and can, therefore, be implemented in a middleware layer. Such a middleware layer could be used to reduce the complexity for application developers which we have seen in section 9.1. For this purpose, we presented a middleware solution running on the same machines as the application servers accessing the datastore. Such a middleware solution can create the client-side illusion of Causal Consistency (section 9.2).

Finally, we discussed how Consistency Benchmarking results can be used to both increase the efficiency of such a middleware solution and to offer further guarantees beyond MRC and RYWC, possibly resulting in a very transparent decision on the trade-offs of consistency versus latency and consistency versus availability (section 9.3).

Part IV.

Conclusions

This Part shall conclude this thesis by recapitulating and discussing the main contributions of our work and future research directions. For this purpose, we start in chapter 10 with a summary of the original problem statement from chapter 1 before revisiting our main contributions and summarizing this thesis.

Finally, in chapter 11, we discuss strengths and limitations of our contributions. We also point out directions for future research and describe ongoing research endeavors.

10. Summary

Today, EC has found widespread adoption in cloud storage services and NoSQL systems. Still, EC is also a very weak consistency guarantee which only promises convergence of replicas after an undefined period of time. Due to this, EC also covers a very broad range of consistency behavior so that the precise degree of (in-)consistency of eventually consistent storage systems is unknown.

Based on this situation, we have identified three main problems in section 1.1 of chapter 1:

- Since EC also shifts the burden of conflict resolution and inconsistency handling from the storage system to the application developer, this unknown behavior significantly increases the complexity of inconsistency handling and, therefore, aggravates application development. Concise knowledge on consistency behavior, in contrast, enables application developers to handle inconsistencies much more efficiently.

- Due to the way consistency behavior impacts application design, awarding consistency as a system quality a level of concern comparable to performance, availabaility, and cost is of paramount importance. Application developers should, therefore, also consider consistency behavior during the selection and deployment optimization of eventually consistent distributed storage systems. This, obviously, requires detailed knowledge on consistency behavior of eventually consistent distributed storage systems deployed in a variety of configurations.

- Finally, different design decisions of storage developers and systems researchers affect consistency behavior in different ways. For some implementation variants, thus, improvements of consistency behavior could be possible without affecting performance or availability. Such an improvement would lead to a pareto-efficient [76] situation but requires the necessary means to study how different system design decisions affect consistency behavior of eventually consistent distributed storage systems.

To address these three problems, we have introduced the concept of Consistency Benchmarking, i.e., the analysis of consistency behavior via both modeling and simulation, as well as system benchmarking experiments. We have also presented approaches for the handling of inconsistencies based on Consistency Benchmarking results. This leads to the following four main contributions:

- *Concise and Meaningful Consistency Metrics:* We have identified and discussed consistency metrics from literature, selected appropriate ones, and developed new consistency metrics which express consistency behavior of eventually consistent storage systems for all consistency perspectives, dimensions and models, in a precise way, without needless aggregations, and in a way that is meaningful to application developers, storage system developers, and systems researchers. This novel set of consistency metrics can be used to describe consistency behavior when studying the impact of design decisions on consistency behavior, when selecting and optimizing storage systems and their deployment configurations, and when communicating concise information on consistency behavior to application developers. Existing related work has so far not addressed the concept of consistency metrics explicitly but rather uses implicitly defined consistency metrics [98, 46, 81, 6, 103].

- *Modeling and Simulation of Consistency Behavior:* We have identified key influence factors on consistency behavior of eventually consistent distributed storage systems and combined them into a model. In a next step, we have presented two distinct approaches which predict consistency behavior based on simulations running on top of this model. These simulation-based approaches can be used to provide fast and inexpensive approximations for consistency behavior, especially when comparing large numbers of storage systems and their deployment configurations or when studying the impact of system design decisions. Existing related work is, due to implicit assumptions, applicable to only a few storage systems and essentially a small subset of our contributions [11].

- *System Benchmarking of Consistency Behavior:* As simulations are inherently limited in their accuracy, we have also presented system benchmarking approaches to accurately measure consistency behavior of eventually consistent distributed storage systems via experiments. These approaches comprise system benchmarks for different consistency perspectives, dimensions, and models as well as for studying different influence factors so that they can be used to verify findings from simulations or to measure unknown behavior. We, therefore, believe that these system benchmarks provide the necessary means: first, to systems researchers or storage system developers who want to determine the precise impact of system design decisions on consistency behavior of eventually consistency distributed storage systems; second, to application developers who want to compare and select different deployment and configuration options of various storage systems; third, to application developers who want to identify the precise consistency behavior of the eventually consistent storage system they are using so that they can handle inconsistencies in a much more efficient way. Existing related work can only detect a few kinds of inconsistency [98] or uses consistency metrics which make the approach inapplicable to the problems which we have identified [46, 81, 6].

- *Inconsistency Handling:* We have also demonstrated how inconsistencies can be handled outside of the storage system leveraging detailed knowledge on consistency behavior of eventually consistent distributed storage systems. For this purpose, we have discussed – based on an exemplary use case – how applications can handle inconsistencies while making use of information on consistency behavior and guarantees. Based on the concept that the resolution of some inconsistencies does not require application-specific knowledge, we have then (for this specific group of inconsistencies) presented a middleware-based approach which guarantees client-centric consistency externally to the storage system. We have also demonstrated how extensions to such a middleware can increase the efficiency of inconsistency handling or offer additional consistency guarantees based on Consistency Benchmarking results. When using these approaches, parts of the complexity of inconsistency handling could then be shifted from the application developer to a middleware component, thus, alleviating application development. Existing related work does so far not use Consistency Benchmarking results and can only guarantee causality which is explicitly defined by applications instead of an existing consistency model [10].

In this thesis, we started with an introduction and background information in Part I, covering different consistency definitions, perspectives, dimensions and models, as well as consistency trade-offs, select storage systems and different kinds of failures which can occur in distributed (storage) systems. In chapter 3, we then discussed related work to demonstrate for each of our contributions their novelty and their progress beyond the state-of-the-art.

Afterwards, in Part II, we introduced the concept of Consistency Benchmarking. We, first, identified requirements for consistency metrics as well as discussed potential metric candidates before selecting and developing appropriate consistency metrics according to the requirements. Next, in chapter 5 we proposed a novel modeling approach to describe the replication strategies and deployment of eventually consistent distributed storage systems. Based on this model, we demonstrated how both calculating convolutions as well as Monte Carlo simulations can be used to predict consistency behavior of such a storage system. Then, in chapter 6, we presented approaches to accurately measure consistency behavior using experiments with distributed storage systems provisioned both as a black-box service or as self-hosted storage system.

In Part III, we have then demonstrated that our Consistency Benchmarking approaches can be implemented and work correctly as well as that their results are helpful and can be used in the handling of inconsistencies. For this purpose, we, first, presented our proof of concept implementations for all approaches from Part II in chapter 7 and discussed their features and limitations.

Next, in our experimental evaluation (chapter 8), we introduced Ministorage as a testbed for our simulations and showed that data-centric consistency behavior can be predicted accurately and that client-centric behavior can be analyzed at least qualitatively – limited by our rather simple client implementation within the modeling tool which is not sufficiently precise for correct quantitative predictions. Next, we experimentally studied the relationship between data-centric and client-centric staleness in Ministorage via system benchmarking, reported the results of a long-term study with Amazon S3, and described how geo-replication and system workload affect the consistency behavior of Apache Cassandra and MongoDB.

Finally, in chapter 9, we described how the example application of an e-commerce webshop can handle inconsistencies based on application-specific knowledge, application design with the datastore in mind, as well as Consistency Benchmarking results. Afterwards, we demonstrated how middleware systems external to the storage system can guarantee MRC and RYWC, i.e., the client-side illusion of CC, discussed how such an implementation could become more efficient based on Consistency Assessment results and what future extensions might look like.

11. Discussion and Outlook

As we have already seen in the last chapter, this thesis is the first work that holistically addresses Consistency Benchmarking of eventually consistent distributed storage systems as well as the use of the knowledge gained by this. While we have presented major contributions in this area, we still see many possibilities for future work in each of our three main directions due to current limitations of our contributions. In the following we discuss limitations of our contributions and directions for future work to resolve them. We also describe ongoing work in this area.

Modeling and Simulation of Consistency Behavior: Our modeling and simulation approach can so far provide quantitative results for data-centric staleness as well as qualitative results for client-centric staleness, MRC and RYWC. As already discussed in chapter 7, this is due to the fact that, for our implementation, we have used a rather simplistic client workload model which severely limits the precision of our client-centric predictions as these heavily depend on client behavior. Here, future work should develop a much more detailed workload model which can be used to accurately model actual application workloads so that client-centric predictions can become much more accurate.

An additional analysis module might also calculate what worst-case client-centric staleness behavior looks like based on a parameterized model and known data-centric staleness results from simulation. We believe that this problem could be solved by combining our Monte Carlo simulation results with the approach of calculating convolutions. Another analysis module might calculate output for the metrics used by the system benchmarking approach of HP Labs [6, 46, 81].

We also see room for improvement in our data gathering tools presented in chapter 7: It is yet unclear how best to measure a distribution of processing times in replicas. Since we have already seen effects from varying processing times depending on the replication strategy and deployment chosen, future work should also analyze whether using distributions of processing times is a good abstraction level or whether there are additional influence factors which should be included in our model.

System Benchmarking of Consistency Behavior: We believe that our system benchmarking approach for consistency measurements is relatively complete and mature. Still, we see much future work in the integration within a tool suite. For instance, as already outlined in chapter 7, our framework for comprehensive system benchmarking is still missing important components, e.g., a failure generator, which can then be used to further study experimentally how the objectives of these components (in our example: failures) affect consistency behavior. Therefore, there are also many open research questions which require running experiments to better understand influence factors on consistency behavior.

Furthermore, our proof of concept implementation could benefit from being firmly integrated into well-established system benchmarking tools like YCSB [33] instead of the loosely coupled integration the other way around. This way, consistency would be measured as well whenever someone runs a system benchmark of a storage system, leading to more mainstream adoption of system benchmarking of consistency behavior.

Handling Inconsistencies: While our middleware implementation guaranteeing MRC and RYWC has been implemented and tested, our prototype does not yet include any of the extensions which we presented in chapter 9. More work is needed to actually use Consistency Benchmarking results in that prototype to increase the efficiency of the solution. It would also be interesting to merge it with the alternative approach by Bailis et al. [10] with the ultimate goal of actually guaranteeing CC not only per key but also for multiple keys.

Furthermore, while we have presented – based on the use case of a webshop – how inconsistencies can be handled within applications, this is a single example only. We believe that future work might be able to decouple this from the concrete use case by identifying a use case-independent application engineering approach for the handling of inconsistencies within arbitrary applications or at least classes of applications. In this direction, much more research is needed.

We also see potential directions in the co-design of middleware and storage systems: Primitives like test-and-set can be provided with little or no overhead within the storage system but greatly ease the handling of inconsistencies within a middleware layer. Systems like PNUTS [32] already implement some primitives – additional ones should be identified and implemented in existing and future storage systems. We are planning to work in this direction.

Ongoing Work: Motivated by the extensive changes in consistency behavior of Amazon S3 (see chapter 8) as well as the fact that an application developer is unlikely to note these changes directly, we have recently published [18] first steps towards continuous monitoring of consistency behavior in a cost-efficient way.

Continuously running system benchmarks is expensive since these system benchmarks are at least time-consuming but typically also expensive in terms of monetary cost. So, instead of continuously running system benchmarks, we have proposed to monitor business key performance indicators (KPI) which are directly affected by changes in consistency behavior – a concept which we call *Indirect Consistency Monitoring* (ICM). ICM will not detect all (especially minor) changes in consistency behavior, instead only business-relevant changes will be noted. While this could be seen as a weakness of the approach, we actually see it as a strength since changes that do not matter to the application developer or provider will just be filtered out. Whenever one or more (depending on the configuration of ICM) KPIs change, a system benchmark of the storage system is automatically triggered to analyze whether the root cause behind the KPI is actually a change in consistency behavior or whether it was a false positive. An example for such a KPI in our webshop scenario from chapter 9 would be the rate of overselling, i.e., the frequency of selling more products than the ones on stock.

We are currently working on ICM to also add tool support, to identify a standard set of potential KPIs which can be reused in many scenarios, to identify sensitivity thresholds for such a set of KPIs, to automate system benchmark deployment, etc.

Closing Remarks: All in all, we have developed and presented major contributions both for the benchmarking of consistency behavior in eventually consistent distributed storage systems as well as the handling of inconsistencies outside of the storage system in contrast to the more traditional approach of handling them within the storage system.

Bibliography

[1] D. Abadi. Problems with cap, and yahoo's little known nosql system. *http: //dbmsmusings.blogspot.de/2010/04/problems-with-cap-and-yahoos-little.html (accessed Jun 27,2013)*, 2010.

[2] D. Abadi. Consistency tradeoffs in modern distributed database system design: Cap is only part of the story. *IEEE Computer*, 45(2):37–42, Feb. 2012.

[3] L. Abraham, J. Allen, O. Barykin, V. Borkar, B. Chopra, C. Gerea, D. Merl, J. Metzler, D. Reiss, S. Subramanian, J. L. Wiener, and O. Zed. Scuba: Diving into data at facebook. *Proceedings of the VLDB Endowment*, 6(11):1057–1067, Aug. 2013.

[4] A. Adya, W. J. Bolosky, M. Castro, G. Cermak, R. Chaiken, J. R. Douceur, J. Howell, J. R. Lorch, M. Theimer, and R. P. Wattenhofer. Farsite: Federated, available, and reliable storage for an incompletely trusted environment. In *Proceedings of the 5th Symposium on Operating Systems Design and Implementation (OSDI)*, OSDI '02, pages 1–14, New York, NY, USA, 2002. ACM.

[5] M. Ahmad, G. Neiger, P. Kohli, J. Burns, and P. Hutto. Causal memory: Definitions, implementation and programming. Technical report, Georgia Institute of Technology, Georgia, Atlanta, 1994.

[6] E. Anderson, X. Li, M. A. Shah, J. Tucek, and J. J. Wylie. What consistency does your key-value store actually provide? In *Proceedings of the 6th Workshop on Hot Topics in System Dependability (HOTDEP)*, HotDep'10, pages 1–16, Berkeley, CA, USA, 2010. USENIX Association.

[7] M. Aslett. What we talk about when we talk about newsql. *http://blogs.the451group.com/information_management/2011/04/06/ what-we-talk-about-when-we-talk-about-newsql/ (accessed Jul 3,2013)*, 2011.

[8] P. Bailis. When is "acid" acid? rarely. *http://www.bailis.org/blog/ when-is-acid-acid-rarely (accessed Jun 15,2013)*, 2013.

[9] P. Bailis, A. Fekete, A. Ghodsi, J. M. Hellerstein, and I. Stoica. The potential dangers of causal consistency and an explicit solution. In *Proceedings of the 3rd Symposium on Cloud Computing (SOCC)*, SOCC '12, pages 22:1–22:7, New York, NY, USA, 2012. ACM.

[10] P. Bailis, A. Ghodsi, J. M. Hellerstein, and I. Stoica. Bolt-on causal consistency. In *Proceedings of the 33rd International Conference on Management of Data (SIGMOD)*, SIGMOD '13, pages 761–772, New York, NY, USA, 2013. ACM.

[11] P. Bailis, S. Venkataraman, M. J. Franklin, J. M. Hellerstein, and I. Stoica. Probabilistically bounded staleness for practical partial quorums. *Proceedings of the VLDB Endowment*, 5(8):776–787, Apr. 2012.

[12] J. Baker, C. Bond, J. C. Corbett, J. Furman, A. Khorlin, J. Larson, J.-M. Leon, Y. Li, A. Lloyd, and V. Yushprakh. Megastore: Providing scalable, highly available storage for interactive services. In *Proceedings of the 5th Conference on Innovative Data system Research (CIDR)*, pages 223–234, 2011.

[13] S. Becker, H. Koziolek, and R. Reussner. The palladio component model for model-driven performance prediction. *Elsevier Journal of Systems and Software*, 82(1):3–22, Jan. 2009.

[14] H. Berenson, P. Bernstein, J. Gray, J. Melton, E. O'Neil, and P. O'Neil. A critique of ansi sql isolation levels. In *Proceedings of the 15th International Conference on Management of Data (SIGMOD)*, SIGMOD '95, pages 1–10, New York, NY, USA, 1995. ACM.

[15] D. Bermbach and J. Kuhlenkamp. Consistency in distributed storage systems: An overview of models, metrics and measurement approaches. In V. Gramoli and R. Guerraoui, editors, *Networked Systems*, volume 7853 of *Lecture Notes in Computer Science*, pages 175–189. Springer Berlin Heidelberg, 2013.

[16] D. Bermbach, J. Kuhlenkamp, B. Derre, M. Klems, and S. Tai. A middleware guaranteeing client-centric consistency on top of eventually consistent datastores. In *Proceedings of the 1st International Conference on Cloud Engineering (IC2E)*, IC2E '13, pages 114–123, Washington, DC, USA, 2013. IEEE Computer Society.

[17] D. Bermbach and S. Tai. Eventual consistency: How soon is eventual? an evaluation of amazon s3's consistency behavior. In *Proceedings of the 6th Workshop on Middleware for Service Oriented Computing (MW4SOC)*, MW4SOC '11, pages 1:1–1:6, New York, NY, USA, 2011. ACM.

[18] D. Bermbach and S. Tai. Benchmarking eventual consistency: Lessons learned from long-term experimental studies. In *Proceedings of the 2nd International Conference on Cloud Engineering (IC2E), to appear.* IEEE, 2014.

[19] D. Bermbach, L. Zhao, and S. Sakr. Towards comprehensive measurement of consistency guarantees for cloud-hosted data storage services. In R. Nambiar and M. Poess, editors, *Performance Characterization and Benchmarking*, volume 8391 of *Lecture Notes in Computer Science*, pages 32–47. Springer International Publishing, 2014.

[20] C. Binnig, D. Kossmann, T. Kraska, and S. Loesing. How is the weather tomorrow?: Towards a benchmark for the cloud. In *Proceedings of the 2nd International Workshop on Testing Database Systems (DBTEST)*, DBTest '09, pages 9:1–9:6, New York, NY, USA, 2009. ACM.

[21] M. Brantner, D. Florescu, D. Graf, D. Kossmann, and T. Kraska. Building a database on s3. In *Proceedings of the 28th International Conference on Management of Data (SIGMOD)*, SIGMOD '08, pages 251–264, New York, NY, USA, 2008. ACM.

[22] E. Brewer. Podc keynote. *http://www.cs.berkeley.edu/~brewer/cs262b-2004/PODC-keynote.pdf (accessed Jun 27,2013)*, 2000.

[23] J. Brzezinski, C. Sobaniec, and D. Wawrzyniak. From session causality to causal consistency. In *Proceedings of the 12th Euromicro Conference on Parallel, Distributed and Network-Based Processing (PDP)*, pages 152–158, Feb 2004.

[24] J. Brzezinski, C. Sobaniec, and D. Wawrzyniak. Session guarantees to achieve pram consistency of replicated shared objects. In R. Wyrzykowski, J. Dongarra, M. Paprzycki, and J. Wasniewski, editors, *Parallel Processing and Applied Mathematics*, volume 3019 of *Lecture Notes in Computer Science*, pages 1–8. Springer Berlin Heidelberg, 2004.

[25] F. Chang, J. Dean, S. Ghemawat, W. C. Hsieh, D. A. Wallach, M. Burrows, T. Chandra, A. Fikes, and R. E. Gruber. Bigtable: A distributed storage system for structured data. In *Proceedings of the 7th Symposium on Operating Systems Design and Implementation (OSDI)*, OSDI '06, pages 205–218, Berkeley, CA, USA, 2006. USENIX Association.

[26] Y. Chen and R. Sion. On securing untrusted clouds with cryptography. In *Proceedings of the 9th Workshop on Privacy in the electronic society (WPES)*, pages 109–114. ACM, 2010.

[27] H. Chihoub, S. Ibrahim, G. Antoniu, M. Pérez, et al. Consistency in the cloud: When money does matter! Technical report, INRIA, 2012.

[28] H.-E. Chihoub, S. Ibrahim, G. Antoniu, and M. S. Perez. Harmony: Towards automated self-adaptive consistency in cloud storage. In *Proceedings of the 13th International Conference on Cluster Computing (CLUSTER)*, CLUSTER '12, pages 293–301, Washington, DC, USA, 2012. IEEE Computer Society.

[29] G. Chockler, R. Guerraoui, I. Keidar, and M. Vukolić. Reliable distributed storage. *IEEE Computer*, 42(4):60–67, Apr. 2009.

[30] A. Cockcroft and D. Sheahan. Benchmarking cassandra scalability on aws - over a million writes per second. *http://techblog.netflix.com/2011/11/ benchmarking-cassandra-scalability-on.html (accessed Dec 10,2013)*, 2011.

[31] E. F. Codd. *The relational model for database management: Version 2.* Addison-Wesley, Reading, Mass., 1990.

[32] B. F. Cooper, R. Ramakrishnan, U. Srivastava, A. Silberstein, P. Bohannon, H.-A. Jacobsen, N. Puz, D. Weaver, and R. Yerneni. Pnuts: Yahoo!'s hosted data serving platform. *Proceedings of the VLDB Endowment*, 1(2):1277–1288, Aug. 2008.

[33] B. F. Cooper, A. Silberstein, E. Tam, R. Ramakrishnan, and R. Sears. Benchmarking cloud serving systems with ycsb. In *Proceedings of the 1st Symposium on Cloud Computing (SOCC)*, SOCC '10, pages 143–154, New York, NY, USA, 2010. ACM.

[34] J. C. Corbett, J. Dean, M. Epstein, A. Fikes, C. Frost, J. J. Furman, S. Ghemawat, A. Gubarev, C. Heiser, P. Hochschild, W. Hsieh, S. Kanthak, E. Kogan, H. Li, A. Lloyd, S. Melnik, D. Mwaura, D. Nagle, S. Quinlan, R. Rao, L. Rolig, Y. Saito, M. Szymaniak, C. Taylor, R. Wang, and D. Woodford. Spanner: Google's globally-distributed database. In *Proceedings of the 10th Symposium on Operating Systems Design and Implementation (OSDI)*, OSDI'12, pages 251–264, Berkeley, CA, USA, 2012. USENIX Association.

[35] G. Coulouris, J. Dollimore, and T. Kindberg. *Distributed Systems : Concepts and Design.* Addison-Wesley, 2nd edition, 1994.

[36] J. Dean and S. Ghemawat. Mapreduce: Simplified data processing on large clusters. In *Proceedings of the 6th Symposium on Operating Systems Design and Implementation (OSDI)*, OSDI'04, pages 10–10, Berkeley, CA, USA, 2004. USENIX Association.

[37] G. DeCandia, D. Hastorun, M. Jampani, G. Kakulapati, A. Lakshman, A. Pilchin, S. Sivasubramanian, P. Vosshall, and W. Vogels. Dynamo: Amazon's highly available key-value store. In *Proceedings of 21st Symposium on Operating Systems Principles (SOSP)*, SOSP '07, pages 205–220, New York, NY, USA, 2007. ACM.

[38] P. J. Denning and J. P. Buzen. The operational analysis of queueing network models. *ACM Computing Surveys*, 10(3):225–261, Sept. 1978.

[39] J. Elson and J. Howell. Handling flash crowds from your garage. In *Proceedings of the USENIX Annual Technical Conference (ATC)*, ATC'08, pages 171–184, Berkeley, CA, USA, 2008. USENIX Association.

[40] C. J. Fidge. Timestamps in message-passing systems that preserve the partial ordering. In *Proceedings of the 11th Australian Computer Science Conference (ACSC)*, volume 10, pages 56–66, 1988.

[41] A. Fikes. Storage architecture and challenges. *https://static.googleusercontent. com/external_content/untrusted_dlcp/research.google.com/en//university/relations/ facultysummit2010/storage_architecture_and_challenges.pdf (accessed Jul 3,2013)*, 2010.

[42] A. Fox and E. A. Brewer. Harvest, yield, and scalable tolerant systems. In *Proceedings of the The 7th Workshop on Hot Topics in Operating Systems (HOTOS)*, HOTOS '99, pages 174–, Washington, DC, USA, 1999. IEEE Computer Society.

[43] S. L. Garfinkel. An evaluation of amazon's grid computing services: Ec2, s3, and sqs. Technical report, Harvard University, 2007.

[44] S. Ghemawat, H. Gobioff, and S.-T. Leung. The google file system. In *Proceedings of the 19th Symposium on Operating Systems Principles (SOSP)*, SOSP '03, pages 29–43, New York, NY, USA, 2003. ACM.

[45] S. Gilbert and N. Lynch. Brewer's conjecture and the feasibility of consistent, available, partition-tolerant web services. *ACM SIGACT News*, 33(2):51–59, June 2002.

[46] W. Golab, X. Li, and M. A. Shah. Analyzing consistency properties for fun and profit. In *Proceedings of the 30th Symposium on Principles of Distributed Computing (PODC)*, PODC '11, pages 197–206, New York, NY, USA, 2011. ACM.

[47] R. Guerraoui, B. Garbinato, and K. R. Mazouni. The garf library of dsm consistency models. In *Proceedings of the 6th European SIGOPS Workshop: Matching Operating Systems to Application Needs (EW)*, EW 6, pages 51–56, New York, NY, USA, 1994. ACM.

[48] R. Guerraoui and C. Hari. On the consistency problem in mobile distributed computing. In *Proceedings of the 2nd International Workshop on Principles of Mobile Computing (POMC)*, POMC '02, pages 51–57, New York, NY, USA, 2002. ACM.

[49] P. Helland and D. Campbell. Building on quicksand. *Proceedings of the 4th Conference on Innovative Data Research (CIDR)*, 2009.

[50] J. M. Hellerstein, M. Stonebraker, and J. Hamilton. *Architecture of a database system*, volume 1. Now Publishers Inc, 2007.

[51] M. P. Herlihy and J. M. Wing. Linearizability: A correctness condition for concurrent objects. *ACM Transactions on Programming Languages and Systems*, 12(3):463–492, July 1990.

[52] H. Hermanns, U. Herzog, and J.-P. Katoen. Process algebra for performance evaluation. *Theoretical Computer Science*, 274(1-2):43–87, 2002.

[53] IEEE. Standard 1061-1998, standard for a software quality metrics methodology. 1998.

[54] H.-A. Jacobsen, P. Lee, and R. Yerneni. View maintenance in web data platforms. Technical report, CSRG No.599, University of Toronto, 2009.

[55] C. Kaner and W. P. Bond. Software engineering metrics: What do they measure and how do we know? In *Proceedings of the 10th International Software Metrics Symposium (METRICS)*, 2004.

[56] M. Klems, D. Bermbach, and R. Weinert. A runtime quality measurement framework for cloud database service systems. In *Proceedings of the 8th International Conference on the Quality of Information and Communications Technology (QUATIC)*, pages 38–46, Sept 2012.

[57] M. Klems, M. Menzel, and R. Fischer. Consistency benchmarking: Evaluating the consistency behavior of middleware services in the cloud. In P. Maglio, M. Weske, J. Yang, and M. Fantinato, editors, *Service-Oriented Computing*, volume 6470 of *Lecture Notes in Computer Science*, pages 627–634. Springer Berlin Heidelberg, 2010.

[58] D. Kossmann, T. Kraska, and S. Loesing. An evaluation of alternative architectures for transaction processing in the cloud. In *Proceedings of the 30th International Conference on Management of Data (SIGMOD)*, SIGMOD '10, pages 579–590, New York, NY, USA, 2010. ACM.

[59] S. Kounev. Performance modeling and evaluation of distributed component-based systems using queueing petri nets. *IEEE Transactions on Software Engineering*, 32(7):486–502, July 2006.

[60] T. Kraska, M. Hentschel, G. Alonso, and D. Kossmann. Consistency rationing in the cloud: Pay only when it matters. *Proceedings of the VLDB Endowment*, 2(1):253–264, Aug. 2009.

[61] T. Kraska, G. Pang, M. J. Franklin, S. Madden, and A. Fekete. Mdcc: Multi-data center consistency. In *Proceedings of the 8th European Conference on Computer Systems (EUROSYS)*, EuroSys '13, pages 113–126, New York, NY, USA, 2013. ACM.

[62] T. Kraska and B. Trushkowsky. The new database architectures. *IEEE Internet Computing*, 17(3):72–75, May 2013.

[63] S. Krishnamurthy, W. H. Sanders, and M. Cukier. An adaptive framework for tunable consistency and timeliness using replication. In *Proceedings of the 32nd International Conference on Dependable Systems and Networks (DSN)*, DSN '02, pages 17–26, Washington, DC, USA, 2002. IEEE Computer Society.

[64] J. Kubiatowicz, D. Bindel, Y. Chen, S. Czerwinski, P. Eaton, D. Geels, R. Gummadi, S. Rhea, H. Weatherspoon, W. Weimer, C. Wells, and B. Zhao. Oceanstore: An architecture for global-scale persistent storage. *ACM SIGPLAN Notices*, 35(11):190–201, Nov. 2000.

[65] A. Lakshman and P. Malik. Cassandra: A decentralized structured storage system. *SIGOPS Operating Systems Review*, 44(2):35–40, Apr. 2010.

[66] L. Lamport. On interprocess communication. *Springer Distributed Computing*, 1(2):86–101, 1986.

[67] L. Lamport. The part-time parliament. *ACM Transactions on Computer Systems*, 16(2):133–169, May 1998.

[68] L. Lamport. Paxos made simple. *ACM SIGACT News*, 32(4):18–25, 2001.

[69] C. Li, D. Porto, A. Clement, J. Gehrke, N. Preguiça, and R. Rodrigues. Making geo-replicated systems fast as possible, consistent when necessary. Technical report, MPI-SWS, 2012.

[70] H. Li and S. Venugopal. Using reinforcement learning for controlling an elastic web application hosting platform. In *Proceedings of the 8th International Conference on Autonomic Computing (ICAC)*, ICAC '11, pages 205–208, New York, NY, USA, 2011. ACM.

[71] W. Lloyd, M. J. Freedman, M. Kaminsky, and D. G. Andersen. Don't settle for eventual: Scalable causal consistency for wide-area storage with cops. In *Proceedings of the 23rd Symposium on Operating Systems Principles (SOSP)*, SOSP '11, pages 401–416, New York, NY, USA, 2011. ACM.

[72] P. Mahajan, L. Alvisi, and M. Dahlin. Consistency, availability, and convergence. Technical report, TR-11-22, Computer Science Department, University of Texas at Austin, 2011.

[73] S. Müller, D. Bermbach, S. Tai, and F. Pallas. Benchmarking the performance impact of transport layer security in cloud database systems. In *Proceedings of the 2nd International Conference on Cloud Engineering (IC2E), to appear*. IEEE, 2014.

[74] T. M. Özsu and P. Valduriez. *Principles of Distributed Database Systems*. Prentice Hall, Inc., Englewood Cliffs, NJ, 1991.

[75] J. Paluska, D. Saff, T. Yeh, and K. Chen. Footloose: a case for physical eventual consistency and selective conflict resolution. In *Proceedings of the 5th Workshop on Mobile Computing Systems and Applications (HOTMOBILE)*, pages 170–179, Oct 2003.

[76] V. Pareto. *Manuale di economia politica*, volume 13. Societa Editrice, 1906.

[77] S. Patil, M. Polte, K. Ren, W. Tantisiriroj, L. Xiao, J. López, G. Gibson, A. Fuchs, and B. Rinaldi. Ycsb++: Benchmarking and performance debugging advanced features in scalable table stores. In *Proceedings of the 2nd Symposium on Cloud Computing (SOCC)*, SOCC '11, pages 9:1–9:14, New York, NY, USA, 2011. ACM.

[78] A. Popescu. Consistency in the acid and cap perspectives. *http://nosql.mypopescu. com/post/4373459618/consistency-in-the-acid-and-cap-perspectives (accessed Aug 1,2013)*, 2011.

[79] D. Pritchett. Base: An acid alternative. *Queue*, 6(3):48–55, May 2008.

[80] T. Rabl, S. Gómez-Villamor, M. Sadoghi, V. Muntés-Mulero, H.-A. Jacobsen, and S. Mankovskii. Solving big data challenges for enterprise application performance management. *Proceedings of the VLDB Endowment*, 5(12):1724–1735, Aug. 2012.

[81] M. R. Rahman, W. Golab, A. AuYoung, K. Keeton, and J. J. Wylie. Toward a principled framework for benchmarking consistency. In *Proceedings of the 8th Conference on Hot Topics in System Dependability (HOTDEP)*, HotDep'12, pages 8–8, Berkeley, CA, USA, 2012. USENIX Association.

[82] R. Ramakrishnan. Cap and cloud data management. *IEEE Computer*, 45(2):43–49, Feb. 2012.

[83] P. Reiher, J. Heidemann, D. Ratner, G. Skinner, and G. Popek. Resolving file conflicts in the ficus file system. In *Proceedings of the USENIX Summer Technical Conference (USTC)*, USTC'94, pages 12–12, Berkeley, CA, USA, 1994. USENIX Association.

[84] S. Sakr, L. Zhao, H. Wada, and A. Liu. Clouddb autoadmin: Towards a truly elastic cloud-based data store. In *Proceedings of the 9th International Conference on Web Services (ICWS)*, ICWS '11, pages 732–733, Washington, DC, USA, 2011. IEEE Computer Society.

[85] M. Satyanarayanan, J. J. Kistler, P. Kumar, M. E. Okasaki, E. H. Siegel, and D. C. Steere. Coda: A highly available file system for a distributed workstation environment. *IEEE Transactions on Computers*, 39(4):447–459, Apr. 1990.

[86] V. Schmidt. Wahrscheinlichkeitstheorie. *http://www.mathematik.uni-ulm.de/ stochastik/lehre/ws03%5F04/wr/skript/node38.html (accessed Jul 12,2013)*, 2003.

[87] A. W. Services. Summary of the amazon ec2 and amazon rds service disruption in the us east region. *https://aws.amazon.com/de/message/65648/ (accessed Aug 16,2013)*, 2011.

[88] A. Singla, U. Ramachandran, and J. Hodgins. Temporal notions of synchronization and consistency in beehive. In *Proceedings of the 9th Symposium on Parallel Algorithms and Architectures (SPAA)*, SPAA '97, pages 211–220, New York, NY, USA, 1997. ACM.

[89] M. Stonebraker, S. Madden, D. J. Abadi, S. Harizopoulos, N. Hachem, and P. Helland. The end of an architectural era: (it's time for a complete rewrite). In *Proceedings of the 33rd International Conference on Very Large Data Bases (VLDB)*, VLDB '07, pages 1150–1160. VLDB Endowment, 2007.

[90] A. S. Tanenbaum and M. v. Steen. *Distributed Systems : Principles and Paradigms*. Pearson, Prentice Hall, Upper Saddle River, NJ, 2nd edition, 2007.

[91] D. Terry. The impact of eventual consistency on application developers. *http://littlemindslargeclouds.wordpress.com/2013/09/27/the-impact-of-eventual-consistency-on-application-developers/ (accessed Jan 13,2014)*, 2013.

[92] D. Terry, A. Demers, K. Petersen, M. Spreitzer, M. Theimer, and B. Welch. Session guarantees for weakly consistent replicated data. In *Proceedings of the 3rd International Conference on Parallel and Distributed Information Systems (PDGC)*, pages 140–149, Sep 1994.

[93] D. B. Terry, M. M. Theimer, K. Petersen, A. J. Demers, M. J. Spreitzer, and C. H. Hauser. Managing update conflicts in bayou, a weakly connected replicated storage system. *ACM SIGOPS Operating Systems Review*, 29(5):172–182, Dec. 1995.

[94] R. H. Thomas. A majority consensus approach to concurrency control for multiple copy databases. *ACM Transactions on Database Systems*, 4(2):180–209, June 1979.

[95] F. Torres-Rojas and E. Meneses. Convergence through a weak consistency model: Timed causal consistency. *Clei Electronic Journal*, 8(2), 2005.

[96] F. J. Torres-Rojas, M. Ahamad, and M. Raynal. Timed consistency for shared distributed objects. In *Proceedings of the 18th Symposium on Principles of Distributed Computing (PODC)*, PODC '99, pages 163–172, New York, NY, USA, 1999. ACM.

[97] W. Vogels. Eventually consistent. *ACM Queue*, 6(6):14–19, Oct. 2008.

[98] H. Wada, A. Fekete, L. Zhao, K. Lee, and A. Liu. Data consistency properties and the trade-offs in commercial cloud storages: the consumers' perspective. In *Proceedings of the 5th Conference on Innovative Data Systems Research (CIDR)*, pages 134–143, January 2011.

[99] M. Welsh, D. Culler, and E. Brewer. Seda: An architecture for well-conditioned, scalable internet services. In *Proceedings of the 18th ACM Symposium on Operating Systems Principles (SOSP)*, SOSP '01, pages 230–243, New York, NY, USA, 2001. ACM.

[100] C. M. Woodside, J. E. Neilson, D. C. Petriu, and S. Majumdar. The stochastic rendezvous network model for performance of synchronous client-server-like distributed software. *IEEE Transactions on Computers*, 44(1):20–34, Jan. 1995.

[101] G. Young. Quick thoughts on eventual consistency. *http://codebetter.com/gregyoung/ 2010/04/14/quick-thoughts-on-eventual-consistency (accessed Jun 21,2013)*, 2010.

[102] H. Yu and A. Vahdat. Design and evaluation of a conit-based continuous consistency model for replicated services. *ACM Transactions on Computer Systems*, 20(3):239–282, Aug. 2002.

[103] K. Zellag and B. Kemme. How consistent is your cloud application? In *Proceedings of the 3rd Symposium on Cloud Computing (SOCC)*, SOCC '12, pages 6:1–6:14, New York, NY, USA, 2012. ACM.

[104] L. Zhao, A. Liu, and J. Keung. Evaluating cloud platform architecture with the care framework. In *Proceedings of the 17th Asia Pacific Software Engineering Conference (APSEC)*, pages 60–69, Nov 2010.

List of Abbreviations

CC	Causal Consistency
CRUD	Create-Read-Update-Delete
EC	Eventual Consistency
GFS	Google File System
HDFS	Hadoop Distributed File System
LIN	Linearizability
MRC	Monotonic Read Consistency
MTBF	Mean Time Between Failures
MTTR	Mean Time To Repair
MWC	Monotonic Write Consistency
NoSQL	Not only SQL
NTP	Network Time Protocol
ODTT	One-Way Data Transfer Time
P2P	Peer-to-Peer
QoS	Quality of Service
RAID	Redundant Array of Independent Disks
RDBMS	Relational Database Management System
RTT	Round Trip Time
RYWC	Read Your Writes Consistency
SC	Sequential Consistency
SLA	Service Level Agreement
SQL	Structured Query Language
WFRC	Write Follows Read Consistency
YCSB	Yahoo! Cloud Serving Benchmark

List of Figures

List of Tables

Index